President [...]

with best wishes

Joe Cronin

STUDENT LOANS:

RISKS AND REALITIES

STUDENT LOANS: RISKS AND REALITIES

Edited by

JOSEPH MARR CRONIN
SYLVIA QUARLES SIMMONS

Massachusetts Higher Education
Assistance Corporation

 Auburn House Publishing Company
Dover, Massachusetts

Library of Congress Cataloging in Publication Data

Student loans.

  Bibliography: p.
  Includes index.
  1. Student aid.   2. Student aid—United States.
3. Student loan funds—United States.   I. Cronin,
Joseph M.   II. Simmons, Sylvia Quarles.
LB2337.3.S88   1987   378'.362   87-1275
ISBN 0-86569-165-7

Printed in the United States of America

CONTENTS

FOREWORD

United States Senator Robert T. Stafford

Massachusetts led the colonies in developing the public concept of universal education in the 1600s. In 1837 Mount Holyoke College, the first college in the country devoted to the education of women, was established in South Hadley. In 1839 Framingham became home to the first teachers college in the country. In that same year Massachusetts' native son, Horace Mann, often called the father of public education, was appointed the first state commissioner of education in the country. In 1861 the Massachusetts Institute of Technology was established and soon became, in 1862, the first land grant college and has set a tradition of excellence in the sciences acknowledged throughout the world. And, finally, 1986 marked the 350th anniversary of the establishment of one of the most prestigious institutions of higher education in this country, Harvard University, which—along with the other fine public and private higher educational institutions in Massachusetts—has made profound and significant contributions to our nation's well-being. In short, Massachusetts' higher educational institutions have led in the development of a system of higher education in the United States that is without equal in any other nation, and educational leaders in Massachusetts have worked hard to provide all of its citizens with access to education—not only the typical student, but also students with special needs.

Those who deal with higher education issues so often focus on day-to-day crises that they sometimes forget the important nature of education and its true purpose. Throughout history, higher education institutions and the learning opportunities they offer have been revered by many nations and cultures. Visionary leaders wanting to build the strength of their nations have always focused on bolstering the educational attainment and literacy of their people, even in states that are not democratic. Conversely, those who have sought to destroy other nations have always attacked the centers of learning and culture in order to reduce resistance to conquest.

For Americans, higher education is an opportunity which, over the last two hundred years, has promised a better life. When the state of Massachusetts was first founded, only those from the most privileged backgrounds were given the opportunity to attend colleges or universities. Subsequently many institutions were created to address gaps in opportunity, most notably a number of fine women's colleges. In recent years, a new set of institutions have been financed, ranging from the University of Massachusetts to the community college system which serves many students who would not be able to attend a four-year residential school.

Indeed, higher education is a form of "big business" in the state of Massachusetts. Many students come from other states in search of a special New England experience. One of the catalysts of Massachusetts' remarkable economic growth has been the human resources provided by its many postsecondary institutions which have facilitated the high tech boom that has been credited with keeping Massachusetts' unemployment rates low. The economy of Vermont has benefited from this technology explosion as well.

Nothing is more important to American society in particular and to a democratic society in general than educational opportunity. In that vein, the availability of Pell grants and Guaranteed Student Loans for today's students makes a discussion about educational quality and opportunity relevant to everyone. The federal government and state guaranty agencies have formed an important partnership that provides access to higher education for countless students.

Surely, when the Massachusetts Higher Education Assistance Corporation was created 30 years ago, its founders pondered these questions: How can we help more people reach their goal of higher education? What is the role of the state in providing assistance to improve the skills of the workforce? How can students from low-income families gain the education they need to improve their economic status? And, finally, how can we help Massachusetts residents develop individual talents to improve their overall quality of life?

These are questions that everyone interested in the future of higher education in this country must take time to consider. Secretary of Education William Bennett recently addressed a forum of Florida educators on the importance of educational quality in America. He elucidated the primary tasks that we as Americans expect our schools to perform: first, instruction that allows each student to reach his or her highest potential; second, a curriculum that provides everyone with a common sense of our remarkable heritage; and third, a teaching force that both models and instills values of honesty, generosity, and loyalty. These three goals outline an immense challenge for all public and private educational institutions.

Unfortunately, these essential and compelling questions are many times overlooked in our struggle to deal with the most immediately pressing problems before us. Recent events regarding the reauthorization of the Higher Education Act serve as a good example of this phenomenon. For over two years, both the House and the Senate have prepared for the reauthorization of the Higher Education Act. I had the privilege of serving as chairman of the Senate Subcommittee on Education, Arts, and Humanities with Claiborne Pell, former chairman of the subcommittee, as my ranking member. Senator Pell and I agree on most issues in higher education. Despite this good relationship and the number of hearings held, we seem to have spent most of our time during this reauthorization reacting to crises rather than reflecting on the appropriate federal role in higher education. I expect that this is true of my House colleagues, as well as the members of the Appropriations Committees of both houses, who are frequently called on to deal with education issues. For example, by the time we have temporarily fixed the problems arising from the Pell grant shortfall, we have lost the opportunity to examine how the program has changed in the past ten years or to determine whether it has been effective in reaching the right students.

Those who work with state guaranty agencies deal most directly with the nuts and bolts issues of student financial aid.

These efforts are directly affected by the debates and the decision making of the Congress. At the heart of the congressional debate throughout the recent reauthorization has been the question of student borrowing in the guaranteed student loan program. Alarm about increased student indebtedness has surfaced repeatedly since the 1980 reauthorization; it is a topic that commands the attention of lenders, educators, policymakers, and the public. Opinions vary, and everyone claims to be the expert. But the issues here are complex. How much should students be able to borrow in order to attend the higher educational institution of their choice? Does a certain level of indebtedness predetermine a student's career choice? Is the spectre of huge college debts keeping certain students out of school? Do students have easy access to educational credit? Should all students have such easy access to guaranteed student loans? Do the mechanisms set up over the past 30 years to administer the GSL program and provide educational credit work efficiently?

My views on these and other issues are strongly influenced by the experience of students, parents, loan officers, college administrators, and state guaranty agency officials in my own state of Vermont. For most Vermont students, access to the GSL program is absolutely essential to help meet their college expenses. Vermont has some of the most expensive public and private schools in the nation. Without the Guaranteed Student Loan Program, higher education would simply be out of reach for many Vermont students, and this is no doubt also true in Massachusetts and elsewhere.

An example of the importance of the guaranteed loans and the need for stability in the program was clearly demonstrated in 1981 when the Administration announced plans to dramatically cut back on GSL availability. Even though those proposals were not enacted by the Congress, the publicity they engendered caused such confusion that many students and their parents feared they would lose their loans before completing college. At one Vermont institution, almost a third of the incoming students forfeited their deposits and did not attend school. In the follow-up interviews conducted by shaken college officials, these students said that without GSLs and other student aid they could not attend college. An even worse possibility for these students was to complete two years of school, owe the government $5,000, and then not be able to get loans to complete their studies.

The current GSL program works in the state of Vermont. In Massachusetts the GSL program is a tremendous success; in fact, Massachusetts has led the nation in innovations to increase access to student aid by needy students. Massachusetts institutions share many similarities with Vermont institutions: They are costly, competitive, and play an important role as focal points in the communities in which they are located.

The Congress is convinced that the GSL program works. One recommendation for improvement was voiced repeatedly during the reauthorization: Increase the loan limits. Although the cost of education has more than doubled since 1976, GSL limits have remained constant. For many students—particularly middle-income students—GSLs are the only form of student aid available. These students have watched their choice of colleges shrink, while opportunities for wealthy students have grown and grant aid for low-income students has increased.

The members of the conference committee have agreed to modest loan limit increases for freshmen and sophomores of $125 annually. Sophomores and juniors will be able to borrow up to $4,000 annually. Graduate students will now be able to borrow up to $7,500 each year. These limits increase as students demonstrate greater commitment to completing their education and, therefore, greater likelihood of repayment. Conferees agreed to these increases despite concern about too much student indebtedness. Only once during the conference was a proposal made to keep the loan limits in current law. The House members suggested a delay of one year in implementing the increased loan limits in order to meet the mandatory cost saving continued for the GSL program in the First Budget Resolution. The Senate conferees roundly and unanimously rejected this suggestion for two reasons. First, we feared that if these increases were delayed by the authorizing committees for one year, then next year the budget committees would attempt to scuttle the increases permanently. Second, our members felt that the time had come to stop cutting student aid first when we have to reduce costs in this program. We made alternative suggestions about where to get savings in the program, specifically by reducing the banks' profits in GSLs. Other suggestions made by the House, such as requiring a guarantee agency fee, were also eventually adopted by the conferees, but the recommendation to delay the loan limit increases was defeated.

Certainly, many students have borrowed more than they should, particularly students from low-income families. This year we have tried to address this borrowing in a number of ways. First, schools will be required to determine Pell grant eligibility before any loans are made. Second, the grant award limits in both the Pell and SEOG programs have been increased, which will offset the need for loan assistance for the neediest students. The maximum Pell grant award will increase to $3,100 by F/Y 1991. The SEOG maximum will be increased to $4,000 annually.

As arduous as the task of reauthorization has been, I am heartened by the deep commitment to higher education that has been reiterated by MHEAC members. Budgetary constraints have meant that guaranty agencies and lenders have had to tighten their belts, but ways have been found to increase grant and loan support for students. The insightful Massachusetts forefathers would be proud of the job being done today to assist Massachusetts students in their pursuit of the higher education they so value. This book, made possible by Massachusetts Higher Education Assistance Corporation, is yet another illustration of the commitment to education in the state. Bringing together concerned and informed voices is a sure way to broaden the current characterization of student borrowing and, further, to offer a practical roadmap for the future.

PREFACE

The Massachusetts Higher Education Assistance Corporation (MHEAC) began as a totally private loan insurance corporation in 1956. The legislature of Massachusetts authorized the incorporators of the new non-profit institution to raise money by subscription or sale of stock, property, or bonds to provide a guarantee for education loans and to do "whatever else necessary to help students, parents, or higher education institutions." Some of the founders wanted the state itself to provide the loan guarantees, but because of negative experiences with state guarantees of railroad stock in the late nineteenth century, the Massachusetts constitution had been changed to prohibit assumption of risk for private debt. One state senator asked the Federal Reserve Bank to take some of the risk, but the federal government—until 1965, ten years later—was not ready to participate in any reinsurance of bank loans for students.

MHEAC celebrated its twenty-fifth anniversary in 1981 with an annual report, a dinner, and publication of a diary of the first twenty-five years. The diverse trustees reflected the organization's widespread support—Cabots and Lowells, college deans, bankers, insurance executives, labor leaders, and state officials of all races and ethnic groups. The education loan program grew in size to $1 billion in 1981 and $2 billion in 1984, and will reach $3 billion in 1987 in Massachusetts. Seven hundred thousand students have borrowed to attend 1,500 institutions of higher education not only in Massachusetts and the U.S. but in sixty nations around the world. Since 1981 the PLUS loan program has provided more than $100 million to parents and, in recent years, to graduate and professional school students in Massachusetts and other states.

In the course of the 1980s, the MHEAC Board has discerned

a need for a "family" of organizations with supportive or related
purposes:

1. *Education Loan Services, Incorporated (ELSI):* a computer and collection services corporation, taxable and for-
   profit, created initially to help secondary markets track
   and service education loans but now serving dozens of
   lenders from origination to final payment.
2. *New England Education Loan Marketing Corporation
   (Nellie Mae):* a secondary market and source of liquidity
   for lenders in Massachusetts and other states; as of 1986, a
   source of one-half billion dollars in education funds.
3. *The Education Resources Institute (TERI):* the holding
   company for ELSI, fiscal agent for the Higher Education
   Information Center, and guarantor of family education
   loans for those who need more than the federal programs
   can provide.

MHEAC has also welcomed the assistance of the Student
Loan Marketing Association (Sallie Mae) and recognized the
availability of tax-exempt loan funds from the Massachusetts
Education Loan Authority (MELA). Members worked with the
previous Board of Higher Education in estimating the need for
additional scholarship funds and assisted the Massachusetts
Board of Regents of Higher Education in processing applications
for state scholarships through 1986. Since 1966 MHEAC has
worked with the U.S. Office, now the U.S. Department of
Education, on every program of education loans where the
guarantee and cooperation of state not-for-profit agencies was
deemed useful. In 1982 MHEAC assisted the Independent
School Association of Massachusetts and Rhode Island in creating PLEASE loans (Parent Loans for Elementary and Secondary
Education) and The Education Fund as an independent guarantor. MHEAC assisted the Boston Plan for Excellence in the
Public Schools in 1985–1986 with the creation of the ACCESS
program of counseling and scholarships for Boston Public High
School students, expanding a modest $30,000 a year program
begun by the Greater Boston Chamber of Commerce into a $5
million endowment program under The Boston Plan.

The original legislative charter granted a life of 50 years to
MHEAC—to most, a very leisurely sunset provision. However,
a medical student beginning a program in 1986 would, under

new federal proposals, have until 2023 to pay back an education loan of $40,000 or more. The Great and General Court passed a bill, which the Governor signed in November 1986, repealing the 50-year limit and extending "perpetual succession to the corporate name," a license to guarantee education loans as long as the members and the legislature remain satisfied with the programs offered.

MHEAC officers in 1986 determined that the thirtieth anniversary deserved not so much *celebration* but *cerebration*—debate and deliberation about the present and future prospects for higher education loan programs. They wanted to present for review the new student loan counseling and debt management model prepared in cooperation with lenders and campus financial aid officers. They also wanted to give the federal government a chance to describe the new provisions for education loans and for collecting from defaulters affluent enough to qualify for a tax rebate. The MHEAC Thirtieth Year Conference achieved those objectives, and this volume includes the major presentations and reports presented on September 19, 1986.

The Conference also provided an opportunity to listen to three recent research reports: (1) how the vast majority of students do repay their loans; (2) how four other industrialized nations structure grant, student subsidy, and education loan programs; and (3) a discussion of the frontiers of education assistance, especially for adult, part-time, and non-traditional students.

Education loans may now be entering a new phase. Parents will increase their support of students by extending their tuition payment terms through loans. We support programs of supplementary loans for education purposes and believe that PLUS and TERI loans are important vehicles to achieve these objectives. These essays, reports, and proposals are intended to enrich the debate over higher education finance in the United States and elsewhere.

JOSEPH MARR CRONIN
SYLVIA QUARLES SIMMONS

ACKNOWLEDGEMENTS

No government report, no recent public policy analysis, has acknowledged the constructive role of student loans and the substantial majority of students subsequently making repayment to education lenders. The Commonwealth of Massachusetts, home of the early Puritan schools and colleges, was also the first state formally to encourage private lenders to invest their funds in young students with no credit rating, no income stream, and uncertain futures. This was risky business, but corporations, foundations, and colleges in 1956 joined in an effort to raise private funds sufficient to absorb the likely risks of death, disability, and default. The decision to do so was made in 1956, and the first loan under the Higher Education Loan Program was disbursed in the spring of 1957.

What have we learned in thirty years of managing a guaranteed student loan program? What is the record of student repayment? How does the American experience compare with that of other mature industrialized nations? Why are we not yet content with student loans, with the accessibility of financial aid to low-income students and minorities? Should students bear the full brunt of paying for college through work and loans, or could parents pay—or borrow—more of the costs, and on what terms? What obligations do colleges and guarantors have to provide information on debt management to young graduates from college or specialty schools?

These are the questions addressed by two hundred and fifty program participants in Boston on September 19, 1986. The idea of a conference was proposed by Sylvia Simmons, Senior Vice President of the Massachusetts Higher Education Assistance Corporation and a former university administrator. The objective was not so much to celebrate the accomplishments of the past as to highlight the central questions of education lending and student finance. Participants included college and university presidents, federal officials, lenders, aid officers, The College Board, legislators, and guarantors from seven states. The major papers presented at the conference appear in edited form in this volume. Senator Robert T. Stafford, Chairman that year of the Senate Education, Arts, and Humanities Sub-Committee, prepared remarks for the occasion. After the conference, the editors asked several participants to add material on new trends of interest to their presentations for inclusion in the book.

The editors are grateful for the work of Elaine Landry, doctoral student at Harvard University, in planning the conference and managing the transformation of conference proceedings into an interesting book. We appreciate the leadership contributions of Julie Neuber, Dr. Thomas Parker, Connie Foley, Doug White, Barbara Feigen, and others who reviewed and helped revise various versions of the text. We pay tribute to the founders of the Higher Education Loan Program, Senator Phillip Graham and Elmer Cappers, first president of MHEAC, along with Massachusetts Senate President William Bulger and MHEAC Chairman William Craig, all of whom were present at the 30th year conference. We thank the hundred leaders who have served on the MHEAC Board of Directors during the past generation. We acknowledge the substantial contributions of the U.S. Congress and federal education administrators in expanding the original program to tens of millions of students and families.

THE EDITORS

ABOUT THE AUTHORS

Ann S. Coles, director of the Higher Education Information Center, has over twenty years of experience working in programs to ensure the accessibility of higher education to low-income and minority students of all ages. She holds a doctorate from the Harvard Graduate School of Education, where her research focused on the participation of first-generation college attenders and welfare mothers in postsecondary education. Dr. Coles is past president of the New England Association of Educational Opportunity Program Personnel.

Joseph Marr Cronin is president of the Massachusetts Higher Education Assistance Corporation and chairman of the board for the New England Education Loan Marketing Corporation ("Nellie Mae"), Education Loan Services, Inc. ("ELSI"), and The Education Fund. From 1972–1975 he was secretary of educational affairs in Massachusetts, and from 1975–1980 he was state superintendent of education in Illinois. He has taught at Harvard, Stanford, Boston College, and Boston University, and has written more than fifty articles, reviews, and books. He has served as a consultant or reader for the National Endowment for the Humanities, the National Science Foundation, the National Institute of Education, the Stanford Research Institute, the U.S. Department of Education, and Voice of America.

Dolores E. Cross has been president of the New York State Higher Education Services Corporation since 1981. Dr. Cross' appointments prior to joining NYSHESC include vice chancellor of student affairs and special programs at City University of New York and associate professor in education and director of teacher education at Claremont Graduate School in Claremont, California. She has authored articles in the areas of equity and access, individualized instruction, and multi-cultural education, and was editor of the book *Teaching in a Multi-Cultural Society*. Dr. Cross holds a Ph.D. from the University of Michigan. She is an active participant in local, state, and national organizations which strive to expand opportunities and services for underserved populations.

Janice Dorian is vice president and director of financial aid at Mansfield Beauty School, Inc. She is a member of the MHEAC Advisory Committee, the MHEAC Loan Counseling Task Force, and the Massachusetts Association of Accredited Cosmetology Schools legislative committee. Through her current responsibilities and in her role as a trainer and consultant, Ms. Dorian has represented the interests of the proprietary vocational sector. Prior activities have included training for NASFAA's Proprietary/non-traditional aid training program and committee member on NASFAA's Proprietary/non-traditional Committee and Financial Aid Committee. Ms. Dorian holds a B.A. from Simmons College.

Ernest T. Freeman is a veteran of twenty-two years in education loan activities. At the Pennsylvania Higher Education Assistance Agency he was instrumental in implementing one of the nation's first fully automated student loan guarantee processing systems. He has served as vice president at Massachusetts Higher Education Assistance Corporation and at Education Loan Services Incorporated. He has been chairman of the Program Operations Committee and the Program Regulation Committee of the National Council of Higher Education Loan Programs, Inc. In addition to his position as President of The Education Resources Institute, he is a member of the Board of Directors of The Education Fund in Boston.

Richard A. Hastings began his government service in 1967 as a management intern with the Department of Health, Education, and Welfare. He has worked for the National Institutes of Health and the Office of Education's Legislative Office staff, and he was the first director of the Division of Certification and Program Review in the Office of Student Financial Assistance. In 1982 he was promoted to director, Management Service, OSFA. He was most recently chosen to head the newly created Debt Collection and Management Assistance Service in the Office of Postsecondary Education. In 1984 Mr. Hastings was personally honored by President Reagan with the highest award available in the Civil Service, the Distinguished Presidential Rank in the Senior Executive Service.

D. Bruce Johnstone is currently president of the State University of New York College at Buffalo. His past positions

include vice president for administration at the University of Pennsylvania, project specialist for the Ford Foundation, and assistant director of the University of Minnesota Center for Economic Education. Dr. Johnstone earned a Ph.D. in higher education from the University of Minnesota and is the author of numerous publications, the most recent of which is "Sharing the Costs of College: Student Financial Assistance in the U.S., France, Germany, and Sweden," a report for the College Entrance Examination Board.

Richard G. King is a senior fellow of the New England Board of Higher Education (NEBHE). Dr. King has served as vice president for research services at NEBHE and as associate director of admissions and financial aid at Harvard College. He was founding executive director of the College Scholarship Service and assistant director of the College Entrance Examination Board. He has taught at the Harvard Graduate School of Education and the University of Alabama, Birmingham. Mr. King served for ten years as a consultant to the Ford Foundation while a member of Harvard's Center for Studies in Education and Development. He was director of programs at the Museum of Science, Boston, from 1974 to 1983. Mr. King is the author of a cooperative study of Mexican higher education, *The Provincial Universities of Mexico,* and is a founding trustee of the Latin American Scholarship Program of American Universities.

Dennis J. Martin is director of financial aid at Washington University. Until recently, Mr. Martin was the assistant director for research and institutional management for the National Association of Student Financial Aid Administrators, where he edited a national bi-monthly newsletter on student aid issues and monitored research and policy analysis studies in the field of student financial assistance. Prior professional activities include his work as project director for a national study of Guaranteed Student Loan borrowers conducted by NASFAA, as project director for the NASFAA *Encyclopedia of Student Financial Aid,* and as faculty member for the NASFAA/NACUBO sponsored student loan management and collection workshop series. Mr. Martin holds a M.A. from Washington University and a B.A. from Rutgers College.

Theresa J. Orr is director of financial aid at Harvard Medical School. She has sixteen years of experience in student financial aid administration, with prior appointments at Tufts University and Brandeis University. Ms. Orr's professional activities in-

clude her work as chairperson for the MHEAC Loan Counseling Task Force, as a faculty member of the NASFAA/NACUBO student loan management and collection workshops, and as recording secretary, Financial Aid Committee of the Thirteen Medical School Consortium. She is a frequent contributor at meetings and conferences on the topics of student borrowing and student debt management. Ms. Orr holds an M.Ed. from Northeastern University and a B.A. from Brandeis University.

Thomas D. Parker was until 1987 director of planning and research and secretary of the corporation at MHEAC, and is now secretary and treasurer of The Education Resources Institute. He was previously a teacher at Brookline High School and an administrator at Harvard University and Bennington College, and he has served in Washington, D.C. at the National Institute of Education, the Fund for Improvement of Postsecondary Education, and in the Office of the Secretary of Education. He has consulted on issues of education and private enterprise at the Data General Corporation and the General Motors Corporation. He is currently a member of the U.S. Department of Education's Advisory Committee to the 1987 Post Secondary Student Aid Study.

Sylvia Quarles Simmons is senior vice president of Massachusetts Higher Education Assistance Corporation. Her professional experience has included positions as associate vice president of academic affairs at the University of Massachusetts and associate dean of admissions and financial aid, Harvard and Radcliffe Colleges. Ms. Simmons has served as a faculty member at Boston College and Harvard College and as a consultant to the Massachusetts Board of Higher Education, the Educational Testing Service, and numerous scholarship programs and educational institutions. Ms. Simmons holds an M.Ed. from Boston College and a B.A. from Manhattanville College.

The Honorable Robert T. Stafford, chairman of the U.S. Senate Subcommittee on Education, Arts, and Humanities of the Labor and Human Resources Committee, is a Republican from Rutland, Vermont, who has served in Congress since 1961. In 1972 Senator Stafford became the 83rd American—the 27th since 1900—to have been elected by a state as governor, member of the U.S. House of Representatives, and member of the U.S. Senate. Senator Stafford was chairman of the Senate Environment and Public Works Committee and has been a

member of the Subcommittee on the Handicapped and the Senate Veterans' Affairs Committee. Senator Stafford received a B.S. degree from Middlebury College and an LL.B. from Boston University Law School. He also holds honorary degrees from a number of institutions of higher education.

Chapter 1

MYTHS AND REALITIES OF STUDENT INDEBTEDNESS

Joseph Marr Cronin and Sylvia Quarles Simmons

Student indebtedness is one of today's more complicated higher education problems. While everyone agrees that students and parents need access to the funds that loan programs provide, there is concern about the increasing debt burden on our nation's youth. Between 25 and, on some campuses, 50 percent of all postsecondary students seek loan assistance to finance college costs. As tuition, room, and board charges increase, the problem will grow more complex.

Student loan borrowing under federal programs peaked in the early 1980s. As those borrowers began to repay their debts, the number of defaults increased, raising a series of issues. Television and newspapers seem especially fascinated by the prospect of young borrowers walking away from their loans, defaulting on their promissory notes, and forcing the rest of the taxpayers to pay for this bad judgment. The truth is much more positive, but somewhat less newsworthy. Ninety percent of borrowers pay back their education loans with very little prodding; another five percent pay when pursued. Of the remainder, one-third pay when challenged in court or denied credit for other consumer loans, or when the IRS attaches an income tax

1

rebate. In Massachusetts during 1986 the federal education loan default rate was 3.7 percent—a low rate, although not as low as that in Vermont, North Dakota, South Carolina, and at least a dozen other states.

The Truth About Student Loans

As with other complicated issues of our time, there are lingering misconceptions about student indebtedness. It is time to examine the myths about student loans in light of the realities of higher education finance. Citizens, educators, lenders—all taxpayers—need to place in perspective what is happening in the student loan programs.

Much has been written about student debt load and its impact on society, the economy, and the individual. Since the first student loan in 1957, college graduates who have borrowed to pay for college have graduated with some debt, then have both paid that debt and prospered. Let us examine some of the myths.

Myth: Reliance on Borrowing Has Tripled Since 1976, and Almost Every Student Is Financing College on Loans

The College Board, which keeps track of college financial aid, reports the statistics shown in Tables 1-1 and 1-2. Since 1975 education loans have tripled. Grants and scholarships have also increased from two sources, states and the campus, while the federal share of financial assistance has not kept pace with inflation.

Although it is true that loans in 1987 will account for almost half of all the financial aid made available to college students, college loans are used by only 25 percent of all college students. Six million students are *not* borrowing for college. Many are attending public universities, which accommodate up to 90 percent of the college students in many states of the union. Fifty percent of all college students in the nation attend public community colleges,

Table 1-1   Financial Aid (millions of dollars)

	1975–76	1980–81	1985–86 (est.)
NDSL	932	902	770
GSL	2,567	8,031	8,493
PLUS		18	562

SOURCE: *Trends in Financial Aid* (Washington, D.C.: The College Board, 1986).

Table 1-2   Financial Aid (millions of dollars)

	1975	1980	1985
Federal	8,560	14,161	15,367
State	490	801	1,374
Campus	1,435	2,138	3,426
All Aid	10,485	17,100	20,167

SOURCE: *Trends in Financial Aid* (Washington, D.C.: The College Board, 1986).

generally with very low tuition. As few as 10 percent of community college students borrow to pay for education. In short, students continue to rely primarily on family resources (parental contributions and student savings), grants, and relatively low public college tuitions to meet college costs.

Myth: Debt Burdens Have Become Intolerable

Some of the rhetoric about "mortgaged futures" is true, but much of the concern is without merit. Consider Massachusetts as an example. Average student loan amounts for four-year degree students have during the 1970s and 1980s edged up from $3,500 to $8,500, but the percentage of borrowers defaulting in 1986 declined from 5 percent to 3.7 percent.

Attendance at college adds, on the average, $600,000 to the lifetime earnings of a graduate. Accumulation of a debt of $10,000 or $15,000, therefore, for most students is not an excessive burden. On the contrary, it is an extremely astute and productive investment. A report by Dennis Martin and Joseph Boyd (summarized by Dennis Martin in this volume) shows that most students can handle their debt burden. Young workers earning $16,000 or more generally can handle a debt load of $10,000 with payments of $124 a month. Most doctors, scientists, lawyers, and business executives also will be able to manage their educational debt; their advanced degrees qualify them for salaries high enough to repay $20,000 or more in education loans.

Students who drop out, who do not qualify for an average or above average salary, or who borrow and then work in low-paying jobs may have trouble—as may the person in debt who heads a family and supports many dependents. This segment may range from 5 to 10 percent of the borrowing students, but not as high as 25 percent of the 25 percent who do borrow. We should worry about this population, however, as we should about debt burdens for social workers, divinity students, public health workers, and teachers, most of whom may need either loan assistance, a longer repayment period, or—most essential—more adequate pay. Japanese teachers, for example, are paid as well as accountants or engineers—40 percent more than their U.S. counterparts. An accountant or engineer who borrows $12,500 will improve lifetime earnings by a million dollars or more. Japan suffers no shortage of teacher applicants in math or science.

Our nation needs to be more inventive in finding economic solutions for those with the highest debt level. One solution is more adequate starting salaries; another is employer assumption of a portion of the payments on education loans.

Myth: Repayment Plans Are Rigid

The Congress twice has shown compassion for borrowers with higher than average loans. It offered options for consolidation through Sallie Mae in the early 1980s and, as of 1986, through all lenders and guarantors as well. While at Harvard, Jerrold Gibson testified to Congress about one graduate student who had 16 loans from different sources. Now it is possible for a borrower to consolidate two, three, or more loans from as many sources, including banks in different states.

Also, the 1986–1987 consolidation program provides for stretching out payments over a longer period of time for borrowers with debt as follows:

$10,000–$20,000	15 years
$20,000–$40,000	20 years
$40,000 or more	25 years

This "stretch-out" helps borrowers by lowering the monthly payment, a boon to young workers the first few years after graduation. Of course, twenty years later the borrower may be sending his own child to college, so it is sometimes preferable to pay off the loan before the end of a 20-year pay period.

Each borrower must look at loan consolidation terms very carefully. After analyzing the requirement to raise the average rate to 9 percent on consolidated loans, MHEAC recommends that borrowers think twice about consolidating NDSL (campus) loans of 3 or 5 percent with loans of 8 and 12 percent just to reduce the number of checks per month or to extend the payment time frame.

Myth: Debt Prevents Students from Pursuing Public Service Careers

U.S. students do not enjoy the options available to Scandinavians, who can defer loan payments while they receive below-average salaries. However, few citizens other than congressmen and higher education aid specialists know about the following public service deferment possibilities offered U.S. borrowers:

1. Three years in the Peace Corps.
2. Three years in the military.
3. Internships in medicine and public health.
4. Volunteer work in a variety of domestic service associations and antipoverty groups.
5. Three years in the National Oceanographic Atmospheric Administration (NOAA).

Borrowers can, of course, enter public service. Indeed, many elected officials now have paid back their student loans. Many in the military service both participate in educational savings plans and accumulate education benefits. Many units of government have raised professional salaries to attract and retain college graduates. Loans by themselves are not deterrents to landing government, military, or public service jobs.

Myth: Debt Discourages Minorities from Pursuing Education Beyond High School

During the 1960s and early 1970s, it was national policy to encourage minorities to attend college, especially blacks and Hispanics, who were underenrolled proportionate to the rest of the population. During the 1980s, however, minority enrollment has showed a decline nationally. What is the explanation? Is it reliance on education loans, as some have alleged?

Quite possibly loans are a factor, especially for first-time students, but this is not an adequate or total explanation. The historically black colleges complained to the Congress and executives in 1980 that lenders were reluctant to accommodate their students. They subsequently obtained commitments from Sallie Mae, Citibank, and HEAF, a guarantor. Student loan volume then rose 10 to 20 percent at most of the minority schools. The Alabama banks and state loan guarantee agency made their own loan funds available to two minority colleges. Minority students continued to apply to and attend schools at both ends of the spectrum: highly selective schools, such as Harvard and Stanford (30 percent minority), and the trade and proprietary schools, many of which have done an outstanding job in attracting and training minority students.

Why, then, are certain minorities attending college less? First, pressure from the federal government for equal opportunity and affirmative action is no longer applied to the state colleges and many private colleges. Minority student percentages are still published in the *Chronicle of*

Higher Education annually, but not much happens to a school that relaxes its minority recruitment. The ferment of civil rights legislation and advocacy has slowed considerably, and the institutional commitment to recruit and retain minorities in many schools has slackened.

Second, minority youth have other opportunities. According to those who work on educational opportunity problems, both the military and certain businesses are recruiting more heavily talented minority youth. States with a full-employment economy, of course, offer many immediate jobs to minority youth.

And third, press publicity each January stressing budget cuts in student aid may discourage low-income students, especially minorities. Although by August or September the Congress rejects most of these reductions, it may then be too late to correct a widespread public impression that funds are no longer available.

So it is true that minority enrollment has ceased to grow and has even declined at certain schools. It is not at all clear, however, that loans are a cause, for loan money is a financial resource. Though not always the first choice for those attending two- and four-year degree colleges, loans are a part of the financial aid packages accepted by most students.

Myth: There Is a Great Shift from Grants to Loans

Reliance on education loans increased dramatically from 1975 to 1985–1986. The amount borrowed nationally grew from $2 billion to $10 billion. The average amount borrowed by individuals for a four-year degree grew from $2,500 to $6,500 in the public colleges and from $2,500 to $8,500 in private undergraduate instruction.

What are the reasons for this growth in loans? Has it been deliberate national policy to substitute loans for grants, as has happened in the Federal Republic of Germany (see Johnstone chaper) and in the Canadian Province of British Columbia? This spectre troubles those who believe strongly that students from low-income families need grants rather than loans and that they are discouraged from applying to college by the prospect of personal indebtedness. This concern is genuine: Poor people often fear banks and loans, having had negative experiences including foreclosures, repossessions, and bank failures. Elders in certain ethnic families counsel the young in general not to borrow and to go to a low-cost college rather than take out a student loan to go to the school of their choice.

The truth is that Congress and many state legislators have fought very hard to preserve and protect grant programs for low-income families and their children. Congress has *raised* the Basic Educational Opportunity (Pell) grant authorization every five years. During the 1980s it had to fight with the Executive Branch, which sought to require more "self-help," but it won, year after year, battles to provide more funds for Pell grants, for which appropriations rose from $936 million in 1975 to $2,387 million in 1980, and to $3,652 million in 1985. The larger states, for their part, have both held down tuition for public community colleges and state universities and increased state scholarship programs from $490 million to $1,374 million in 1985–1986—for example, in Massachusetts, from $15 million in 1980 to $75 million in 1986, and in New York State, from $200 million to $400 million in 1986.

What financial aid sources, then, have been eliminated or sharply reduced? First, the GI Bill, one of the most popular and productive financial aid programs ever enacted, grew to $4 billion a year in the 1970s, after Vietnam, but is now less than $1 billion a year. Most veterans who wanted education help got it. The armed services today offer a Veterans Education Assistance Program (VEAP) and a new GI Bill which is a blend of savings and educational incentive grants.

The $4 billion was lost not from federal higher education budgets but from Veterans Administration/Defense expenditures. The $4 billion total is always included in 1975 statistics reported by The College Board, an authoritative source on such matters. But this money was never generally available to any college student who had not previously served in the military. It is not now, and never was, part of the Higher Education Act, the U.S. Office of Education budget, or the U.S. Department of Education. It was not cut: It withered from diminished eligibility and appetite after most of the veterans who wanted higher education used the assistance.

A second instance was the Survivor's Insurance part of Social Security, which provided that an orphan or a child of a disabled person who went to college could remain a recipient of up to $2,000 a year until age 21; otherwise, the young person remained eligible only until age 18. This humane and generous provision was repealed by the President and Congress jointly in the deficit reduction actions of 1981, the first and most popular Reagan Administration budget, supported in both houses of the Congress.

Almost two billion dollars were spent for one million college students under Social Security in 1980–1981, but this provision had disappeared by 1986, phased out gradually each year after 1981 until the last eligible survivor graduated or dropped out. At the time it was thought that these students remained eligible for other higher education grants and loans because of low family income. Educators, in fact, knew little about how the Social Security program helped college students. (It covered essential living expenses for thousands of students living at home or in public housing projects.)

Education organizations were concentrating on protecting the higher education budgets, and they did not mobilize substantial support for saving the Social Security provision. As with the G.I. Bill, this loss was not from the federal higher education budget, but it is similarly reported in the College Board tables for 1975. The disappearance of this Social Security/welfare and human service benefit was one more source of discouragement for a low-income 18-year-old torn between the prospect of a job offering ready cash, and a college education that had to be obtained with a loan and without survivor's benefits. This action was not, however, a deliberate shift by Congress from grants to loans. No researcher has yet documented the full impact on city students, on minorities, or on rural students.

To take a different perspective, the surge in education loans can be explained by three separate forces: (1) The Middle Income Student Assistance Act, (2) expansion of the loan program to the states, and (3) extension of eligibility to trade, technical, and proprietary schools. First, Congress supported the Middle Income Student Assistance Act in 1978, the year that it chose "education loans for all" over a tuition tax credit for education that could have been even more expensive. Secretary of HEW Joseph Califano, Congressman William Ford, and others decided that all income groups could qualify for a subsidized below-market loan. They chose this approach rather than entitle every American family to a tax break for their college attendance. During the three years 1978–1981 the Guaranteed Student Loan Program experienced its greatest surge of growth. Some well-to-do families took out loans and invested either in tuition or in high interest money market investments whose values soared at about the same time. This program abuse was stopped by a series of Congressional actions.

By 1981 the Congress had restored an income cap on automatic eligibility, a need test for students in families with more than $30,000 income, and subsequently directed that student loan checks be sent to the school after education need was verified by a college official. Even so, the popularity of "college on credit" grew rapidly and for a time, uncontrollably, and during the three-year period of unusually high inflation, 1980–1983, the cost to the government soared. After 1983 the cost per loan declined as inflation and interest rates moved downward.

In 1976 Congress took a series of actions to stimulate expansion of the loan program to all states. The incentives included cash advances to create an instant loan reserve fund to any state agency, automatic 100 percent reinsurance of defaulted loans for the first five years, and assumption of most administrative costs. This package served to expand the program into states which previously had no agency or private non-profit corporation to promote or stimulate higher education attendance with the help of loans. A substantial share of guaranteed student loan program growth has occurred in the midwestern, far western, and southern states that established loan guarantee agencies between 1977 and 1981. Prior to then, banks in those regions either declined to make education loans or found great frustration in dealing directly with the federal government on Federal Insured Student Loans (FISL), a centralized loan program helping the non-GSL states and schools.

The Congress in the 1970s made trade, technical, and proprietary schools eligible to receive guaranteed student loans. By the early 1980s millions of students attending these schools, some of which offered programs of 600 clock hours or twelve-week certificate courses, qualified for federal student loans. These non-degree schools account for almost one-third of the loans guaranteed by the California agency and more than 10 percent of new loans in many states. Much of the program growth, and a share of student loan defaults, comes from schools and students which for years did not qualify for Pell grants or state scholarships at all. Again, this was not a shift from grants to loans; these schools have only recently won eligibility for education grant programs.

Economists have argued for twenty years that education carries with it benefits for both society and the individual, and that an individual's earning power will be enhanced considerably by college attendance. During the 1970s both the Carnegie Commission on Higher Education and the Committee for Economic Development agreed, therefore, that tuition at public colleges could be charged at one-third of actual cost because of this "individual benefit," personal investment theory.

College officials, even at the best-endowed and most selective colleges, agreed among themselves during the 1970s to a "self-help" financial aid policy wherein: (1) scholarship aid would be spent on larger numbers of needy students rather than concentrated on those with exceptional merit; and (2) the self-help component could consist of student savings and earnings (summer and term-time) and of borrowing from lenders. Therefore, the notion that college students could obtain both grants and loans gained in popularity during the 1970s and 1980s and was justified by the economic reasoning that education was a personal investment as well as a boon to society. In the 1980s, financial aid officers reported that student loans were offered to middle-class families not eligible for need-based grants, and to working-class and low-income families as part of a financial aid "package" of grants, work, and loans. Thus, loan volume grew as some families found themselves eligible only for loans, while others eligible for grants were expected to borrow and work part-time to show an investment in self.

In summary, the GI Bill and Social Security payments have declined or been dropped, Pell grants and state scholarships based on need have increased, and loans have been expanded to more states, to more families, and to schools other than colleges and universities. This interpretation is more nearly descriptive and fairer than the notion that all college students have suffered a massive shift from grants to loans. Low-income families should have more of the education costs paid for by grants, while middle-income families can rely on more loan funds—especially with two in college at once. No student should have to work full time. These are fundamental principles that should drive the debate about "how much in loans, how much work, how much grants."

Myth: The Loan Program Is Too Costly

Maureen Woodhall, the London economist who has analyzed education loan programs in more than fifty countries, concludes that almost every nation makes the mistake of assuming that loan programs are very cheap and that new loans can be made from a revolving fund. Loan programs cost money, and costs may escalate rather than decrease over time.

The U.S. loan program, relying mainly on banks to lend

capital and on the government to pay only for subsidies and defaults, is a very productive program. Three or four billion dollars in government money each year generates nine or ten billion in new loan funds. This three-to-one ratio is popular in that Congress can properly take credit for leveraging two new dollars by paying out only one. The program could be even less expensive, according to analysts in the Office of Management and Budget, if one or more of the following provisions were changed:

1. Eliminate the loan subsidies and charge a market rate to students. In 1986 the Congress decided that the subsidy of interest rates should expire for borrowers five years out of college, cutting the duration of subsidy to students who do not begin to enjoy prosperity until their sixth year of employment.
2. Require the student to pay his own interest or find someone to pay interest for him while he is in college. Congress does not believe that all full-time students can pay interest costs, but reluctantly assesses a 5 percent origination fee which, paid to the lenders, is really in lieu of student interest payments for five to six months. Unfortunately, this fee is deducted from the loan proceeds, creating a discounted loan, all of which must be paid back later.
3. Designate someone else to pay a portion of the defaults—perhaps the lender, or the state, or even the student. Lenders, if pressed to absorb the full risk, would react by lending only to their own good customers or to families with good credit ratings, not to strangers nor to many independent students. During the late 1960s and early 1970s some states did assume 20 percent of the default liability, but others in the southern, western, and central parts of the country declined to participate in such risk. The pledge of 100 percent federal reinsurance eventually persuaded the last fifteen non-participating states to enter the loan program by the early 1980s. States with default rates of more than 5 percent obtain only 90 percent reinsurance; those with a rate of 9 percent or more receive a maximum of 80 percent once they reach that level of defaults each year.

In 1987 the OMB proposed that students themselves pay a 9 percent guarantee fee which would generate a billion dollars, enough to pay the total federal default bill for those who had gone to school and defaulted. In effect, new college students would pay the defaults of their older brothers, sisters, or cousins. The Congress is not likely to accept this creative "user fee" theory without substantial modification.

Woodhall found that it is necessary to raise money for three types of costs for most government loan programs, even if a country relied on banks for the basis capital: (1) payment of defaults, (2) subsidy of low-interest notes for students, and (3) administrative costs for program management. These costs can amount to from one-third to two-thirds of the programs. Loans are not "free"—not if they are below market, not if they are insured so as to reassure lenders to invest in students, and not if a government wants enforcement of loan terms and aggressive pursuit of borrowers at repayment time.

The U.S. Government pays $3 billion a year to generate $9 billion in loans to 3 million students. For every $3,000 of loan aid to students, therefore, the government pays one thousand dollars. If the Congress phased out the loan program and converted the funds to grants, $3 billion would pay for only $3 billion in grants, and students would lose $6 billion in financial aid. That's why parents, students, colleges, and the Congress like the loan program. These simple economic facts are so basic that it is a wonder why more people do not praise the loan program for its leverage, its productivity, and its usefulness to the taxpayer.

So much for the myths and the realities of student loans and higher education finance. What of the future and the various solutions proposed?

The Future of Education Lending

Frequently, the Congress reviews proposals to redesign the entire structure of education loans. Key committees listen to experts and advocates, then decide what to keep, what to reject, and what to launch as an experiment. Congressmen do not want to gamble with higher education. They listen to constituents and select a course with considerable caution.

Recasting a major aid program calls up the insight of H.L. Mencken: "To every complex problem, there is a simple solution—and it is almost always wrong." So it may be with education loans. There is often hope for a better program, but the wise course is to test it before widespread adoption. Following are several major proposals of recent years:

National Student Loan Bank

A National Student Loan Bank in the 1970s was widely acclaimed as the most likely way to assure access to education loans. Minorities, poor people, and operators of technical and proprietary schools complained that loan funds were not available. This situation was true in many states as late as 1980.

The Loan Bank proposal required the federal government to set up a national bank and allow all students to borrow from a central fund. The U.S. Treasurer could either set aside money from the Federal Financing Bank or borrow money, as the U.S. Government does every week. Does the federal government need to assume such a heavy responsibility? The federal experiment with the Federal Insured Student Loan was not encouraging. The default rates for education loans in California and the District of Columbia rose to excessive levels and the delay in paying insurance to lenders was so long as to discredit the program. The federal government eventually added several thousand collectors in regional U.S. offices, potentially effective but terminated by the next administration.

The Loan Bank idea lost its impetus when each and every state established a guarantee agency, when Citibank and Sallie Mae provided funds to minority colleges, and when the California banks agreed once again to make education loans via the GSL program. The national student loan bank may well be an idea whose time has come and gone. In comparison with previous federal loan programs, the GSL program enjoys a lower default rate, high lender confidence, and stability of loan origination and collection activity. It is an example of public-private sector collaboration that appeals to education-minded legislators of both parties.

Federal Income-Contingent Loans for Education

The Reagan Administration offered this proposal to the Congress both in 1986 and 1987. The idea is not new; it was suggested in various forms in the 1950s by Milton Friedman and others. The Ford Foundation sponsored a thorough study in the 1970s and Yale University adopted a Tuition Opportunity Plan (TOP) based on the Ford study.

In brief, the Income Contingent Loan provides undergraduates with all the money they need and, after graduation, sets the repayment level at some percentage of the borrower's income. The Federal Income Contingent Loan for Education (FICLE) proposal in 1986 offered a 15 percent cap on payments and low monthly payments for the first year or two. Various newspapers endorsed it. In 1986 the Congress decided to authorize a $5 million trial of the idea at 10 colleges or universities. Why is an experiment necessary? There are three reasons why it cannot be implemented quickly:

1. The collection concept, although respectful of low-income recipients, requires a great deal of recalculation each year as the income of graduates changes. This requires extensive self-reporting by individuals.
2. Serious issues arise in reporting the income of the self-employed, of business people who plow back earnings into a company, of divorced individuals, and of people who stop working or marry wealthy individuals.
3. While FICLE would appeal to those who enter the ministry or who write poetry, music, or novels for a living, it

seems unlikely that anyone who plans to earn an above-average income would apply for a loan that might cost more than a fixed-rate loan. Also, the 1987 version appeared to require much more of low-income borrowers (up to 15 percent of income), which was viewed as a negative feature by many educators.

The National Association of Student Financial Aid Administrators calculated that a person borrowing $15,000 would pay $5,000 more in interest on a FICLE loan than on a regular student loan. Others worry that FICLE is part of a program to replace grants and subsidized loans with unsubsidized loans of from $10,000 a year up to $50,000 for undergraduates. Such a course would result in further escalation of loan burdens—much more so than the authorized GSL limits of $13,000 for four years and $17,500 for a five-year undergraduate degree.

Home Equity Loans

In 1986 the Congress amended the Higher Education Act of 1965 authorizing parents to borrow $4,000 per student per year in education loans called PLUS (Parent Loans for Undergraduate Students). In rewriting the tax code, Congress repealed the deductibility of interest on consumer loans (including PLUS) but allowed interest deductions on home mortgages, including second mortgages or home equity loans. Will this development persuade some families to borrow on their homes for education, in order to be able to deduct the interest when computing their income tax? The answer is yes: Equity loans will gain in attractiveness, but there will be some limits not yet fully discussed:

1. A smaller proportion of families will itemize deductions in 1987 and 1988.
2. A home equity loan requires a pledge of one's property, drastic action if one needs only $4,000 a year (or less), the PLUS loan maximum.
3. The PLUS loan rates were dropped from 12 to 10 percent for 1987, and may decline further so as to compete with mortgage rates.

4. Not everyone has a house or unpledged home equity, or wants to collateralize an education loan with one's homestead.
5. The Congress may decide to restore tax deductibility for any higher education loan, not just those from home equity loans.

Work Instead of Loans

Prior to World War II, many individuals worked their way through college. In the 1970s and 1980s, however, the federal college work-study option and campus work in general accounted for only 4 percent of higher education assistance. Frank Newman and others have called for a return to emphasis on work of two kinds: (1) public service, from tutoring adult illiterates to providing care for the elderly or mentally ill; and (2) career-related work, including the occupations for which either liberal arts or technical majors might eventually qualify.

Work and college mix well up to a point; college counselors recommend no more than 12 or 15 hours of work per week for a student. Athletes, scientists, and future doctors may not be able to allocate sufficient time to work because of the demands made on them for laboratory work and practice. The Cooperative Education Movement deals with this problem by interspersing months or semesters of work with academic or professional study.

It is important to note that work does not pay for as much of college as it once did. To pay an $8,000 college cost at a minimum wage of $3.50 would require 55 hours of work a week—which shows how preposterous is the old timers' suggestion that one should work one's way through college as they did "in the old days." In fact, loans are an attractive, practical alternative to work: By borrowing $2,000, one can take more courses, graduate early, and increase one's earning power faster. Students who study part time because they work full time often take six to nine years to obtain a bachelor's degree.

Grants

Almost every student (and financial aid officer) wants more scholarship aid, more grants. It would be unreasonable to object in general to this proposal at the national, state, or campus level, but it would be unwise to convert $9 or $10 billion of loans suddenly to $3 billion in grants without thinking of the consequences. Could middle-income students get loans from other sources? Would thousands of students be forced to "trade down" to a less expensive school? In short, what would be the consequences? Can we calculate the impact campus by campus?

Grants are not only more popular but more effective than loans for certain purposes. For example, the freshman year, or first semester, is a time when dropout rates are very high, and withdrawals tend to result in loan defaults. The longer a student stays in school, the less likely he or she is to default. Also, in the case of short-term specialized programs, job placements are often uncertain. Only those who stay in a program more than one month should qualify for a loan.

Parent Loans

The Sloan Commission at MIT in 1980 recommended a major shift in education loans toward parent assumption of debt rather than student loans. The commission also recommended market rate loans rather than subsidized loans. That same year Congress authorized Parent Loans for Undergraduate Students (PLUS) effective January 1, 1981. The potential popularity of this enactment was demonstrated by the Massachusetts parent, who on January 2, 1981, borrowed $3,000 from The Boston Five Cents Savings Bank for the second semester at Simmons College.

Since 1981, however, parent loans have grown slowly. It took twenty years (1956–1976) for popular acceptance of student borrowing, so five years (1981–1986) may not be enough time for acceptance of parent loans at market rates.

In fact, when the early PLUS loan rate of 9 percent rose to 14 percent in 1982, the market response was, predictably, downward. The larger issue, of course, is whether parents should assume a greater share of borrowing for the cost of education. A chapter in this volume examines the rationale and options for parent loans.

Subsidy

Subsidized loans cost money—currently one-half billion dollars for every percentage point up from the Treasury Bill rate. Congress views seriously the issue of excess subsidy for any loan program, whether for housing, farms, shipping, or education, and it will take action to adjust the level of subsidy. Since 1980 the interest rate on National Direct Student Loans has been raised from 3 percent to 5 percent, and the rate on GSL loans has been raised from 7 percent to 9 percent and then, as Treasury bill rates fell, lowered to 8 percent. As the Treasury Bill rate dropped from 1983 to 1986, the amount of subsidy, as well as the percentage of subsidy, dropped substantially from record highs during 1981–1983.

Also, Congress decided that for a student five years out of college, the GSL program rate should rise to market level, or at least to 10 percent, thus curtailing the ten-year subsidy for young professionals. For consolidation purposes a student with loans in excess of $5,000 can consolidate NDSL, GSL, PLUS, and some other government loans, but only with a new rate of at least 9 percent. Again we see a drop of subsidy inasmuch as GSLs in early 1987 yielded an 8.75 percent return to lenders. And, Congress raised the parent loan from 9 percent rate to 14 percent in 1982 as interest rates generally rose, then lowered it first to 12 percent, then to 10 percent in 1987.

Those who worry about great jumps in federal student loan subsidy costs pass too lightly over Congressional willingness to fine-tune, correct, and adjust loan subsidies. A case can be made for even greater loan subsidies—for manpower categories in short supply, for students from the lowest income stratum, for the accomplishment of public purposes such as community service or assistance to the needy. Loan policy thus can serve other social and national needs.

Summary

Unquestionably, young people need more information about loans, debt, the credit system, personal finance, and the consequences of default. The Higher Education Act as amended in 1986 made more explicit the obligation of schools to provide entrance and exit counseling to borrowers. This topic is addressed in greater detail later in this volume. The absence of debt counseling has been a program flaw. Under the NDSL, campuses must provide information on debt repayment; after 1986, GSL borrowers also will obtain this information.

The Guaranteed Student Loan Program is much more successful than most Americans believe. One quarter borrow—far from all students—and most pay it back—more than 90 percent. The program has become more flexible, and costs, along with eligibility, have been reduced. Loans cannot be blamed for the lack of minority applications or for excessive program costs; in fact, loans are extremely cost-effective for government.

Many major changes, such as a loan bank or an income-contingent loan program, are either unnecessary or very difficult to administer. The financial aid future includes more grants, more work, more reliance on parental loans, and more counseling and advice to those who take out education loans. With fine-tuning and adjustments, the partnership of schools, lenders, and guarantors can flourish for years to come.

Section One

THE REPAYMENT OF LOANS

In response to the problem of education loan defaults, several states surveyed the characteristics of student loan defaulters. They discovered that defaulters tend to be people who have not finished a postsecondary program, who live in metropolitan areas, and who are from a below-average income background. However, defaulters include all races and all income groups.

One of the most serious misperceptions is that all defaulters are educated ingrates, people who can afford to pay but who have walked away from their bank obligations and from a supportive government. In fact, as many as half of the defaulters are willing to pay but are unable to do so because of economic or personal misfortune, including physical or mental disabilities, job difficulties, and such family trauma as divorce. Sometimes a defaulter does not earn enough to cover more than the cost of food, clothing, and housing.

There is, however, another substantial group of defaulters who either can pay on schedule or could pay when they are 25 to 27 years of age. Many in this group do make payments when they are reported to national credit bureaus whose reports are made available to home mortgage bankers and providers of credit cards. Young professionals do not want a permanent stain on their credit rating when they find out that eligibility for other loans and entrance to sensitive professional or business or government positions depends on a record of repaying their insured federal loans.

23

A national study by Dennis Martin and Joseph Boyd provided a refreshing picture of those who do, in fact, repay their loans. Sponsored by the National Association of Student Financial Aid Administrators, this study examined the financial capacity of those who entered the repayment stage and measured the amount of stress or strain encountered. This study is the first of a series of needed correctives to counterbalance the occasional articles citing the agony faced by those who, retroactively, wish that their loan were actually a grant.

In the early 1980s the U.S. Congress resolved to harness the combined talents of the U.S. Department of Education and the Internal Revenue Service to pursue defaulters affluent enough to qualify for income tax rebates. During 1985 and 1986, state guarantee agencies were invited to send computer tapes of education loan defaulters to the Department of Education and the IRS. Many of those whose names were submitted had never made any payment, while others had not paid within 180 days. In Chapter 3 Richard Hastings, a senior Department of Education official in charge of debt collection, describes their vigorous and effective efforts to prevent government tax rebates to those who owe the federal government money.

Another strategy is preventive. Chapter 4 discusses loan counseling based on early efforts to advise young borrowers of the existence of debt management strategies. Remarkably, a loan counseling model was developed and agreed upon by financial aid officers representing a wide spectrum of institutions: Harvard Medical School, public colleges, and a family chain of cosmetology schools. Congress supports the strategy of entrance and exit interviews. The financial aid profession needs all possible help and materials to assist in the proper advising of the largely inexperienced borrower signing promissory notes for the first time.

The following chapters extend the frontier of knowledge about those who repay and address the question of how to improve the integrity of education loan programs by counseling on the front end and impoundment of federal tax rebates at the other end.

Chapter 2

REPAYMENT, RESPONSIBILITY, AND RISK

Dennis J. Martin

National Trends

Approximately 12 million people in this country each year participate in postsecondary education.[1] While the demographics and composition of the student body may fluctuate somewhat over time, we can expect a stable enrollment.

The College Board estimates that, in the 1985–1986 academic year, over $20 billion was allocated to student assistance programs at postsecondary institutions in this country.[2] The bulk of this amount (over 76 percent) is federally sponsored dollars. Even in the days of Gramm/Rudman/Hollings and in the face of vast deficits threatening the federal budget, it is clear that federally supported student aid is popular, well supported, and has its place in the priorities of overall national policy setting. Recent findings from the Department of Education's first major attempt to create a research data base on student aid support this observation. The Department found that 51 percent of today's postsecondary students enrolled for six or more credits receive some form of financial assistance. Of those who receive student aid, over 80 percent depend upon some form of federal assistance.[3]

As we look at broad trends, two additional observations are noteworthy. First, costs of attendance have increased at a pace well above inflation.[4] This trend is likely to continue. Even though we have seen stability in the federal role—and certainly not the kinds of cuts in student aid proposed by the Administration each year—the net effect has been an erosion in the purchasing power of the student aid dollar. Adjusting for inflation shows that federal student aid has declined by nearly 10 percent from 1980–1981 to 1985–1986, again using the College Board's estimates.[5] This erosion in purchasing power of the student aid dollar leads us to our last observation on national trends. Student loan borrowing has increased by leaps and bounds in recent years because a gap is created when costs of attendance above inflation rates combine with declining student aid dollars, in a "real" dollar sense.

Exhibit 2-1 examines activity in the GSL program over the six years (1978–1984).[6] In addition to the annual levels rising above $8 billion in 1984, we see the result of actions such as the Middle Income Student Assistance Act (MISAA) of 1978 which expanded GSL eligibility to veritably everyone (note the sharp increases in 1979 through mid-1980). The Omnibus Budget Reconciliation Act of 1981 (note the sharp decline beginning around 1981) repealed MISAA, for all practical purposes, and needs tests were applied to all GSL applicants with family incomes greater than $30,000.

One might have expected the curve to show some leveling off from 1982 to 1984, but student borrowing increased sharply. We see the effects here of increasing college costs, lack of growth, and, indeed, a decline in grant and student work resources with GSLs filling the gap. We also see evidence of the GSL program reaching a point in its maturity where the program is working just as it was intended: as a federally subsidized program, generating significant amounts of private capital to provide loans to students at reasonable terms. Any access problems experienced in prior years have been resolved by widespread lender interest, and today a student wishing to borrow a GSL probably has little trouble getting one (assuming he or

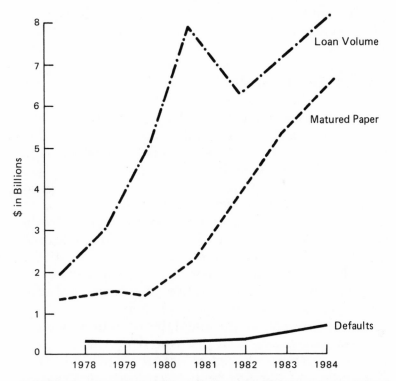

Exhibit 2-1 Guaranteed Student Loans. Annual loan volume, matured paper, and defaults (FY 1978-1984). Includes Plus Loan data.

she otherwise qualifies).* Of course, even in such halcyon days as these—and ironically perhaps because of them— we are not without special problems. The GSL program presents several rather formidable challenges to policyma- kers in the Congress and to the higher education commu- nity generally.

Suffice to say that in the ten-year period between 1975 and 1985, the number of GSL borrowers in this country more than tripled, from an annual figure of less than one million to over three million. The average loan amount

---

*This chapter was written prior to the Reauthorization of the Higher Educa- tion Act, which has since become law. Though it is too soon to tell, initial projections on the effects of the new law suggest a leveling off, perhaps even some decline, in the number of students borrowing and the dollars expended in GSLs. Even so, major (negative) effects on enrollment or access to higher education are not predicted.

nearly doubled ($1,311 per year versus $2,320 per year[7]).
More students borrowed more loans than ever before.

The NASFAA Loan Study

Two hypotheses about student borrowing attract attention.
The first—perhaps a visceral concern but nonetheless
real—is that increased levels of indebtedness will lead to
increased instance of default. The second hypothesis is that
the level of sacrifice required of borrowers to make good on
their commitments to repay forces a variety of choices on
their part, none of which is optimal from the individual's
standpoint or viewed favorably in a societal context. Borrowers may forego the more traditional consumption patterns in lieu of making their student loan payments, or
they may choose more lucrative professions and careers
rather than those that better serve society.

One measure of the growing interest in these matters is
the wide audiences such discussions now attract. Frank
Newman's report on higher education policies, *Higher
Education and the American Resurgence*, describes "excessive" debt burdens as being detrimental to college
persistence, career choice, consumption patterns, and traditional values.[8] The May/June 1986 issue of *Change* magazine focused on student aid issues and, in particular,
student borrowing. The leadline on the cover, "Student
Aid: The High Cost of Living on Credit," with the graphic
portrait of a woman graduate—donned in cap and gown, a
grimly set demeanor, posed behind bars shaped in the
form of a dollar sign—exemplifies some of the recent
interest (and a not-too-subtle bias) that the subject of
student borrowing now fosters.[9] These are but two recent
examples. Those whose concern with student debt levels is
longstanding can find some gratification in the wider play
given to the student debt question. In many respects it has
been a long time coming.

Part of the recent interest is kindled by research efforts
that seek to put to the test some of the theoretical,

philosophical, and occasionally emotional responses which underpin the question, "How much should a student borrow to finance postsecondary costs?" Also, have students been able to repay their loans without an "excessive burden"? The pursuit of this question and a curiosity about the characteristics and attitudes of borrowers led NASFAA to a research project which would explore the characteristics of borrowers who are currently in repayment and in good standing on their loans.[10] After all, the vast majority of borrowers, at least to this point, are able to make good on their commitments. NASFAA hoped to learn from these repayers something of their experiences, to achieve a better understanding of today's borrowers (who are now in school) and tomorrow's borrowers, and the repayment challenges each will face. NASFAA was able to conduct this research as a result of grant support provided by the Lilly Endowment. Under the terms of the grant, Dr. Joseph D. Boyd, a well-known student aid researcher, was contracted to design the research and conduct the study and statistical analysis.

The research involved a survey of 3,000 GSL borrowers in repayment status. The mail survey was conducted in the spring of 1985. Borrowers were selected randomly from the repayment files of 12 states (Arizona, California, Colorado, Florida, Iowa, Illinois, Massachusetts, New York, North Carolina, Oregon, Tennessee, and Texas). In addition to the mail survey, telephone interviews were conducted with 82 randomly selected borrowers. The mail survey produced 628 usable responses, for a 24 percent response rate. The findings are based on these responses.

Several limitations of the research should be kept in mind. First, we surveyed borrowers in repayment status and did not attempt to work with borrowers who had defaulted on their loans. This approach was, of course, intended in the research design, but it should be kept in mind. Second, while the response rate, 24 percent, is similar to that experienced in other research on borrowers in the repayment period, the research did not involve an examination of larger data bases in order to measure the characteristics of respondents in comparison to non-residents, simply because data bases are not available for this purpose.

A response rate of this kind is not adequate to make absolute generalizations about such a vast program as the GSL. However, conclusions can be drawn from the respondents who participated, since they represent a reasonable random sampling of the borrower population. And, while no scientific measure of analogous control groups was built into the study, the findings hold up when compared with Census Bureau data, National Center for Education Statistics reports on enrollment characteristics and participation rates, and other research studies on student loan borrowers. Even with the limitations, there is much to be learned in examining the respondents who participated in the NASFAA study, but these caveats should be kept in mind.

A final caveat is this: the mean year for when repayment started for these respondents is 1982, an important point. This fact leaves open the speculation that the mean debt levels reflected by the borrowers in our study, and consequently their attitudes about loan borrowing and repayment, may be much different from those of borrowers now in the system, or soon to enter repayment, who borrowed in more recent years and therefore would report much higher levels of debt.

In the study, we collected a great deal of information about GSL borrowers and the GSL program. We raised a number of important questions for further examination in what we hope will be an ongoing focus for those doing research on loan programs and the behavior of borrowers. Some of the key findings are as follows:[11]

1. Most of our respondents (79.6 percent) reported using GSL for undergraduate study only. The average total GSL debt for these borrowers was $4,390. When all education loans are considered for this group, the average debt was $5,299.
2. Thirteen percent of our respondents used GSL for graduate study only. The mean GSL debt for these borrowers was $7,235.

3. When GSL's were used for both undergraduate and graduate study, the mean GSL debt was $11,386; 7.5 percent of our respondents used GSLs for both undergraduate and graduate work.

4. Overall, 20 percent of all GSL borrowers in repayment reported also using NDSL. In these cases, the average NDSL was $2,619.

5. Men and women borrow at relatively similar rates, but, as perhaps is not surprising, given various reports on salary discrimination in this country, women report earnings which are considerably lower than men:

   Mean Salaries: $23,093 Men/$17,040 Women ($6,053 Difference)
   Mean GSL Debt: $5,776 Men/$4,097 Women ($1,679 Difference)
   Mean Total Debt: $6,816 Men/$6,232 Women ($584 Difference)

6. On average, women must utilize a greater portion of disposable income than men in order to maintain their loan repayments. Taken in the context of lifetime earnings, one is struck even more by the differences in salaries between men and women. Data from the Census Bureau show that men who graduated from four-year colleges can be expected to earn between $1.2 and $2.75 million in their lifetimes. Women who graduate from four-year colleges are expected to earn between $520 thousand and $1.12 million. The fact that student loans (and GSL in particular) appear to be equally accessible to both men and women gives little solace when one considers the ultimate social context in which loan repayments exist.

7. As one would expect, the average debt burden differs according to type of institution the borrower attended:

   • The Mean GSL at Public College was $4,885.
   • The Mean GSL at Private College was $6,170.
   • The Mean GSL at Trade and Tech Schools was $3,036.

8. Only 10.8 percent of the respondents to our study indicated that parents have in the past or are now helping them to repay student loans. The most likely groups of borrowers to report such help are those whose parents had incomes of $50,000 or more (while the borrower was enrolled), younger borrowers recently out of school, and

those whose parents assisted in meeting college costs while the borrower was in school. But even among these subsets of respondents, only 19 percent reported repayment help from parents.

9. In rating the sources of information about loans, these borrowers rated postsecondary institutions at the top of the scale, followed by the GSL lender, the secondary school, newspaper or magazine articles, state guarantee agencies, and the federal government last. A phenomenon of note among Massachusetts borrowers was that postsecondary institutions ranked first, lenders were a *close* second, and the state agency ranked third (rather than fifth as it did in the national ratings).

10. Of major interest is the ratio of repayment to income examined in non-theoretical terms by borrowers actually in repayment. Some models seek to project the extent to which a level of debt will be manageable, given the variables of starting salaries at the time of repayment, salary increases over the duration of the repayment period, and lifestyles and standards of living. In our research, we had the opportunity to examine in real terms the percentage of income directed toward managing student loan repayments.

11. NASFAA's research found that 5.5 percent of gross, or 7.5 percent of take-home pay, was the average repayment-to-income ratio. Ultimately, this finding is valuable only for borrowers above or below the average; it is especially pertinent since the range, particularly above the mean, is quite large. There were, in fact, borrowers in our study whose loan repayments exceeded 12 percent of gross income. Just over 7 percent of all borrowers experienced such repayment demands. Borrowers who face monthly repayments of $100 or more per month (over 20 percent of the borrowers in NASFAA's study) typically use over 8 percent of gross income to manage repayments. Indeed, some borrowers reported income-to-repayment ratios above 17 percent, and while there were too few in this category to draw meaningful conclusions, it is impressive that no single absolute ratio level can be set as a universal standard of burden.

12. On the other hand, it is important to note that significant numbers of borrowers reported percentages of repayment to gross income well within what might be called a

comfortable range. Just over one-third of the borrowers in this survey, for instance, reported that *less* than 3 percent of gross income was required to manage loan repayments.

Based on NASFAA's research, two major factors seem to define the degree to which loan burden does or does not impact negatively on an individual once repayment has begun: (1) when loan payments exceed $100 per month, and (2) when repayments are 8 percent or more of gross income. Approximately 10 percent of the borrowers participating in the NASFAA study demonstrated these characteristics, and it is for these students that the impact of student debt is the highest.

The impact of loan debt was measured in the study by asking borrowers in repayment to rank responses to a variety of questions that sought to determine the effects of loans on personal, day-to-day decisions. Four particular responses separate the subset of borrowers paying $100 or more per month, with 8 percent or more of gross income, from others. Table 2-1 attempts to show how the impact of student debt can be measured and for whom it is a burden.

Repayers who face monthly payments of $100 or more per month and who must utilize 8 percent or more of their gross income to manage these payments experience the greatest hardships. These are the repayers (an estimated 10 percent of the overall population) who demonstrate the greatest impact of educational debt on personal life decisions. Proportionally, more of these borrowers are women, and most are single. Twice as many more than is the case in the general population have borrowed NDSL in addition to GSL. Debt burdens are relatively high, while gross incomes are relatively low. On average, for this subset, the ratio of repayment to income is nearly 13 percent.

One additional bit of more recent analysis using this data set may be of interest. Joseph D. Boyd has been examining respondents to the survey who reported multiple loans from more than one program or source. While the numbers were small and there is concern about reliability in developing national estimates, some interesting trends are suggested by these respondents. In the respondent popu-

TABLE 2-1   The Impact of Loan Debt: A Three-Way Comparison

		$100 Monthly Repayers	
	All Respondents	Less Than 8% of Gross Income	8%-up of Gross Income
Percentage women	56.1	47.6	60.0
Percentage single	57.7	53.5	81.7
Percentage indicating that employment played a major role (20% or more) in meeting college costs	44.5	47.6	21.7
Percentage also using NDSL loans	20.6	35.7	51.7
Mean NDSL loan(s)	$2,619	$3,203	$3,209
Mean GSL loan(s)	$5,288	$8,467	$8,495
Percentage also borrowing loans from parents	9.0	8.3	20.0
Mean of all loans	$6,488	$10,440	$11,870
Percentage first/only enrollment at private college or university	37.5	51.3	59.6
Mean years used loans	2.59	3.53	3.74
• Considered loans essential	6.90	7.14	7.88
• Loans permitted choice	6.02	6.35	6.47
• Now wished less was borrowed	3.65	2.83	4.92
• Has difficulty handling repayments	3.44	2.96	4.98
• Loan debt caused purchase of used car	3.51	2.96	5.62
• Loan debt affected ability to save regularly	5.01	4.93	7.28
• Annual loan repayments	$987	$1,642	$1,925
• Borrower's gross income	$20,007	$26,592	$16,092
• Borrower's take-home income	$13,884	$17,892	$12,192
• Ratio of mean percentage loan repayments to gross income	5.51	5.77	12.77
• Ratio of mean percentage loan repayments to take-home income	7.49	8.53	16.86

SOURCE: This table first appeared in *Proceedings, College Scholarship Service Colloquium on Student Loan Counseling & Debt Management* (1986).
RATING: 1 is low, 9 is highest.

lation for NASFAA's survey, about 30 percent borrowed from another source in addition to GSL to finance post-secondary education. For these respondents, loan consolidation and income contingent repayments are policy issues very much tied to such questions as how much can be borrowed and from how many sources. It is not surprising that respondents to NASFAA's study who have more than one type of loan expressed a greater desire for loan consolidation than others. Just over 36 percent of those who used GSL and two or more other loans for undergraduate work and 42 percent of those who borrowed similarly for graduate study expressed a desire for a loan consolidation program. These findings compare to roughly 14 percent of those with single-loan sources being interested in loan consolidation. What is somewhat surprising is that those with multiple loans did not express even greater interest— perhaps because of the general unfamiliarity with loan consolidation and the fact that, after all, these are borrowers in repayment who are able to manage things as is.

With regard to income-contingent repayments, a significant majority of respondents with a GSL and two or more other loans (over 60 percent) supported the concept of loan repayments based on annual income and scheduled to increase proportionately as income does. The idea of income-contingent repayments is not new; it was raised in the late 1970s and early 1980s by Dwight Horch, Bruce Johnstone, and others.[12] It is also a concept recently proposed by the Administration in its FY 1987 student aid proposals[13] and included as a pilot program in the Senate's version of the Reauthorization Bill.[14] Despite what are surely challenging administrative concerns to be addressed, there appears to be support, at least among certain kinds of borrowers, for this type of repayment option. It is not desirable or workable for everyone. But as a repayment option or as a plan directed toward specific subsets of the borrowing population, income-contingent repayments may work well.*

---

*Since this chapter was written, the Reauthorization of the Higher Education Act has occurred and the pilot program described is contained in the law. The original pilot suggested in the Department of Education's FY 1987 budget has since become the centerpiece of its FY 1988 budget proposals.

These observations reflect in many ways the overall theme of NASFAA's research: The GSL is a vast program, affecting all kinds of students with all types of needs and attending all types of institutions, in our wonderfully diverse system of postsecondary education. It is not only difficult to generalize about such a program and its impact; from a borrower/consumer perspective it is also difficult to structure policies that do not benefit certain kinds of borrowers at the expense of others. Provisions for loan consolidation or income-contingent repayments, *for certain kinds of borrowers,* provide the kind of targeted flexibility needed for some, but not all.

In summary, NASFAA's loan study emphasizes the foregoing sort of reasoning. When one looks at averages and means, one is struck in observing that for the vast majority of borrowers in repayment today, student loans are not a burden, nor do they affect plans to purchase a house, start a family, or otherwise participate in the American dream. In the same breath, however, we must quickly add that NASFAA's research helps to focus on those who are in fact more negatively affected by student debt than others. In this respect, greater emphasis should be placed on student loan and debt management counseling. Greater awareness generally as to the nature of credit financing is desirable, as perhaps is ultimately student aid packaging policies that seek to address the special needs and characteristics of students as they participate in our diverse system. Key to this, however, is a reaffirmation of the importance and commitment to grant and work resources for students. In recent years—at the national level, at least—the desirable delicate balance among the grant, work, and loan types of student aid has tilted to the loan side of the equation. A recovery of this balance is needed, though perhaps this is an unrealistic hope in today's budget climate.

In any event, student loan programs and other credit financing mechanisms have become central in the payment of college costs. It thus behooves us to learn what works well, what needs remain unaddressed, and what borrowers can tell us of their experiences. This is the kind of knowledge we will require in order to meet the ongoing challenges we face in the financing of postsecondary education.

Reflections on the Massachusetts Experience

In general terms, Massachusetts GSL borrowers have characteristics quite similar to those of their peers in different states who have GSLs. Although the size of the population is too small (only 87 respondents) for meaningful statistical inferences to be drawn, these observations may nevertheless be of some interest:

1. Eighty percent of those who attend a postsecondary institution and have a loan guaranteed by Massachusetts reside in the Commonwealth. The remaining 20 percent are spread out over 12 other states (concentrated mostly in the northeast and mid-Atlantic region), with one respondent living abroad.
2. Men and women borrow in Massachusetts with the same frequency as other respondents.
3. Massachusetts borrowers are, on average, slightly younger than all others (26 years old as compared with 28.5).
4. Far fewer borrowers appear to be married, but this apparent finding may be an aberration of the small response size. Debt levels are somewhat higher ($5,585 versus the overall mean of $4,390 for undergraduate borrowers, for example). Loans are used, on average, for slightly longer periods (over 3 years as compared with about 2.5 in the general response group); and parental incomes during the in-school period appear higher than the general group (by about $5,000).
5. There appear to be more recipients of bachelor's degrees and fewer certificate/associates degree recipients than in the general group. There is greater use of GSLs in private, traditional four-year colleges and less in the public college sector than is the case in the general group. Both of these findings are not surprising and reflect the educational influences prevalent in the Commonwealth.

There are no significant differences along attitudinal lines to be reported. In short, there were no surprises or sharp differences of note when Massachusetts borrowers who participated in our study were separated out and examined. In my view, this observation is significant in itself because Massachusetts is one of the more established and one of the largest of the state GSL operations. Wide variance in the response of Massachusetts borrowers would have cast doubt on the quality of responses by the general group and the meanings attributed to them.

What has Massachusetts done to counsel student borrowers? Nearly ten years ago, Harvard's Richard Kraus, one of the first and most influential thinkers on the implications of student debt, explored ways in which manageable debt levels could be forecast in order to provide students with insights about the ramifications of debt before they found themselves overburdened.[15] In a 1978 publication of the Massachusetts Association of Student Financial Aid Administrators, the question, "How much should I borrow?" was raised and discussed from the student's perspective. This "Guide to Student Borrowing" outlined the terms of repayment, examined the various income potentials by career field, and sought to offer guidance on the proper relationship between income and loan repayment.[16] The document listed 6 percent as the desirable ratio—that is, loan repayments kept within 6 percent of annual income can be managed without pushing limits. While the authors of the 1978 "Guide" took pains to describe their figure as only an estimate to provide general guidelines, their 6 percent estimate model is remarkably close to the actual experiences of GSL borrowers in repayment who participated in NASFAA's study.

These are but two examples of the firm foundation built in the mid- and late 1970s under the leadership of members of the Massachusetts student aid community. Upon this foundation much has been built, and the term "renaissance" is indeed appropriate when one considers the blossoming and awakening that has occurred since these early days. As part of the College Scholarship Service's Colloquium proceedings, in a session titled "Mechanisms That Work," Sylvia Simmons, Senior Vice President of Massachusetts Higher Education Assistance Corporation (MHEAC), discussed an exemplary model whose purpose is to "provide accurate and timely information about credit financing and responsibilities that go along with borrowing for higher education."[17] The model developed by MHEAC is quite unique in its approach but more so in its structure. It utilizes and depends upon a task force structure that brings together lenders, schools, agency personnel, and all parties to the process to work together in a unified way to achieve mutual goals. The ultimate beneficiaries will, of course, be the students of the Commonwealth and their families who, as a result of these efforts, will realize the value of postsecondary education and acquire the responsible attitudes about debt necessary to maintain the kinds of programs available today. It is to be hoped, in the spirit of renaissance, that this model will be adopted by other states as well.

The leadership role of those who live, work, and serve the higher education needs of Massachusetts is clear in these examples. The leadership and innovation continues with such new programs as SHARE and with such new entities as Nellie Mae and TERI, each with roots in Massachusetts.

There will always be *risks* associated with borrowing on the prospects of what a postsecondary education will bring. There will always be *responsibilities* associated with *repayment*. To these three *r*'s I would add two others: We must commit ourselves to the need for ongoing *research* on the characteristics and behavior of borrowers and overall on the impact and effectiveness of student aid programs; and to the *renaissance* of emerging ideas, techniques, and practices that keep us moving forward.

Endnotes

1. National Center for Education Statistics. *The Condition of Education, 1985 Edition* (Washington, D.C., September 1985).

2. Washington Office of The College Board. *Trends in Student Aid: 1980–1986* (Washington, D.C., 1986).

3. Center for Statistics. *National Postsecondary Student Aid Study: Field Test Results* (unpublished draft report, July 1986).

4. Cathy Henderson, "Forecasting College Costs Through 1988–89," ACE Policy Brief (Washington, D.C., March 1986).

5. *Trends in Student Aid: 1980–1986*, op. cit.

6. U.S. Department of Education. *Guaranteed Student Loan Program Data Book, FY-1984* (Washington, D.C., March 1985).

7. National Association of Student Financial Aid Administrators *Student Financial Aid. Making a Lifetime of Difference* (Washington, D.C., 1985).

8. *Chronicle of Higher Education.* Excerpts from Frank Newman's "Higher Education and the American Resurgence" (Washington, D.C., September 18, 1986).

9. *Change, The Magazine of Higher Learning* (Washington, D.C., May/June 1986).

10. Joseph D. Boyd and Dennis J. Martin. *The Characteristics of GSL Borrowers and the Impact of Educational Debt, Volumes I and II* (Washington, D.C., NASFAA, 1985).

11. Dennis J. Martin. "Long-Term Implications of Student Borrowing," in *Proceedings, College Scholarship Service Colloquium* (CEEB, 1986). See also Boyd and Martin, *The Characteristics of GSL Borrowers and The Impact of Educational Debt.*

12. NASFAA. *Student Loans: Alternatives for Reauthorization:* "Student Loans: Some Practical Radical Alternatives," D. Bruce Johnstone; "Estimating Manageable Educational Loan Limits for Graduate and Professional Students," Dwight Horch (NASFAA, 1978).

13. *Budget of The United States Government, FY 1987.*

14. *S. 1965:* Senate version of the Reauthorization of The Higher Education Act.

15. Richard A. Kraus. "Education Loans—How Much Should I Borrow??? A Guide for Graduate and Professional Students," (1979).

16. Massachusetts Association of Student Financial Aid Administrators. "Guide to Student Borrowing" (1978).

17. Sylvia Simmons, panel presentation published in *Proceedings, College Scholarship Service Colloquium on Student Loan Counseling and Debt Management* (CEEB, 1986).

Chapter 3

THE IRS STUDENT LOAN COLLECTION PROGRAM

Richard Hastings

Although concerns about the ability of students to repay education debt have been present throughout the history of student assistance, they have increased in recent years. It is important, therefore, that any discussion of the student loan program include information about affirmative steps being taken to insure public support for higher education. The IRS Student Loan Collection Program is one way of maintaining positive public regard for the management of the program.

The Higher Education Act created the guaranteed student loan program in 1965. It took 14 years to make the first $10 billion in GSLs. Between 1979 and the end of fiscal year 1985 the program increased to well over $50 billion in loans—quadrupling the loan volume in just six short years. Slightly over half of all loans that have been made are currently in the repayment phase. The obvious consequence of this situation is that, if the default rate remains stable (and currently about $1 out of every $10, at least initially, does not go into repayment on schedule), we will have problems over the next few years as those loans reach maturity.

That fairly basic arithmetic has caused Secretary William Bennett to note with some alarm that we are facing the prospect of a billion dollars in the near term and a total of something around $13 billion by the end of the decade if we do not do something about the situation. Clearly we are not talking about commercial experiences here. The old adage, "The loan well made is half repaid," while certainly true in the guaranteed loan program, is not quite as controlling as it would be in other sectors. A billion dollars a year, however, is big money by anyone's accounting.

Addressing the Problem

Over the past few years there have been great efforts to address the default problem. Guarantors and Department of Education staff have looked at possible measures to achieve both improved collection and default prevention. The NCHELP Committee on Default Prevention presentation made in 1984 was extremely influential when Congress considered the guaranteed loan program in reauthorization. Probably three-quarters of the recommendations coming out of that study were in fact adopted either by the House or the Senate and were incorporated into the final bill. The Administration also proposed several measures for fiscal year 1985 which subsequently were enacted as part of the reconciliation process, and their suggestions were also adopted in the reauthorization process.

Finally, the Deficit Reduction Act of 1984 gave us the best collection tool yet—namely, the ability to use, on a pilot basis, the Internal Revenue Service to "offset" federal income tax refunds due individuals who owe money to the United States. In this area, as in so many others, it was state government that led the way. The IRS holds a well-defined view of its role which does not include collecting debts for anybody except the IRS. The persuasive evidence from Oregon, New York, Pennsylvania, and a few other state agencies which have used this approach, however, persuaded Congress—particularly the Senate—that a pilot effort would be worthwhile. In 1985 the IRS joined this venture with five federal agencies; in 1986 it expanded to eight agencies.

The law specifically provides that only debts owed the United States are eligible for collection by the IRS. Since student loans are, in fact, owed the United States, the U.S. government ought to be able to attach refunds. State revenue directors would love to use the same remedy available for their state tax recovery purposes that we are currently using on guaranteed student loans. Given the efficacy of this process, it is almost certain that Congress will review the results and find it in the public interest to have this tool remain available to the federal government—in a controlled fashion.

Concerns and Questions

For its part, the IRS continues to have two concerns, one of which is whether or not people will reduce their withholding rates in order to avoid having a refund. The evidence from the states with experience using revenue procedures for the collection of debts suggests that this does not happen. A study we conducted in 1985 on the collection of defaulted loans looked at that question in two states. We found that a majority of the people who had been offset once (that is, had their refunds docked) were offset again, and that the people who were offset the second time were offset for a greater amount than the first time. I do not know what that finding indicates about human nature—whether it is inclined toward lethargy or inertia—but it appears to be true. In any case, offsetting has not led to extensive willful playing with the system.

The second IRS concern is that nothing in the law says that taxpayers have to give the IRS a tax-free "loan" to begin with. Something like three-quarters of the American people get an income tax refund every year, having made this generous overpayment to the United States, but nothing in the law requires it. On the contrary, the IRS requires only that taxpayers prepay within 20 percent of the actual tax amount and comply with the deadline stipulated by law.

The larger question, and the greater concern (with no

good evidence in hand yet) is whether or not people will cease to file returns altogether. The IRS presented evidence to Ways and Means on its experience in the child support field, the first use of the IRS to collect non-tax debt under a provision fostered by Senator Russell Long when he was chairman of the Senate Finance Committee. The Commissioner suggested that there was some evidence that people whose refunds had been docked tended to be twice as likely not to file a return in succeeding years. But then he went on to say that there really is insufficient evidence on this question. People involved in child support may have many reasons for not filing a return in the subsequent year; family situations tend to be chaotic, and there certainly may be changes in earnings.

The participation of guarantee agencies may require review, and Congress probably ought to address certain due process questions legislatively, since these are federal debts. Due process procedures provide the opportunity for a federal appeal to anyone, even though the debt originates in a guarantee agency. The question of providing adequate notice, however, is another area in which further legislative guidance is needed.

Results of the Program

The federal tax offset in the student loan program has been a tremendous success. In the first year of the program, a total of $126 million was received from the IRS, about a quarter of which ($36 million) was monies related to GSL accounts. In total, those funds came from 236,000 individuals. The average offset was about $540, and 65,000 of those 236,000 were GSL defaulters. In Massachusetts, for example, the Department of Education recovered $1.5 million, offsetting 45 percent of the accounts where the individual was on the IRS taxpayer rolls. The national average, by the way, is 43 percent.

Those are good results. The biggest question, as we study the nature of people who default on loans, has been whether we are dealing with people who do not have the ability to pay or whether we are dealing with people who lack the desire to pay. When nearly half of all defaulters can be offset, somebody out there is earning money. Now $540 may not be much money, but there are other places where those folks would prefer to spend it. These collection results suggest the possibility of a telephone approach to working out a repayment arrangement. Of course, we do not know about the other 57 percent from whom we did not receive any money; GAO will look at them in their study of this process. We do know that they did not get a refund; we do not know whether they had income, and we need an answer to that question.

Three-fourths of all the guarantee agencies who participated last year are fairly well convinced of the benefits of the IRS collection program. In 1986 some 200,000 accounts were turned over by the agencies participating; this year more agencies will turn over more accounts—approximately 700,000 of them. Without the $36 million collected this year through the IRS, the overall default rate in the guaranteed loan program would have been one-half percent higher. Considered as a proportion of the 10 percent default rate, the collection rate looks even better. On a cash flow basis, the present value calculations will be significant. Getting the tax offset into permanent law is a primary objective of the Reagan Administration.

Publishing the names of defaulters is another approach. For example, the Massachusetts State Director of Revenue has decided to publish a list of tax delinquents. In the Eastern District of New York, the U.S. attorney recently filed about 150 judgments in one day, and *The Daily News* ran an article about it on the front page of its first edition. The reporter not only picked up the names and addresses and the amounts owed from court records, but also found the names and addresses of the delinquent employers. The number one person on the list happened to be an attorney working for a Wall Street firm who owed the federal government $26,000, even though he was making $90,000 a year. The day after publication in the press, this account was paid in full.

Federal education officials recognize that there are a

large number of hardship cases. Hopefully, some of the deferment possibilities that are being proposed in reauthorization will handle some of these needless defaults. But there are far too many people who clearly have the ability to pay and simply are choosing not to do so because it has not been made worth their time and effort in the past. With the new provisions that have been enacted into law, I think we can convince borrowers that it is worth their while to deal with us. These allowances include passing along to defaulters all costs associated with the collection of these loans, raising the interest rate to market rate, and imposing penalty interest. Additionally, required credit reporting is now going to be the single most effective tool outside of the use of the IRS.

The federal government began reporting NDSL student loan defaults to credit reporting agencies in the fall of 1984. Six weeks after we sent out 60-day notices to people telling them that we were going to report them to credit agencies, Education Department collections jumped by a million dollars a month. That increment has remained in collections for almost two years now. Every week we get phone calls from people who are refinancing or buying a home and who have been caught on the credit report. Usually we are able to move them to get a consolidated loan, amortized over 30 years, and nobody ever knows about it. The interest rate is sometimes higher, but this strategy solves their problem.

Related to credit reporting, though, is the requirement that we now report the existence of all loans to credit bureaus. This requirement is going to be extremely beneficial to the more than 90 percent of people who are honoring their commitments by making repayments as scheduled. In fact, these payments will give them a positive credit history, which many of them do not have because they have done no other borrowing. Another useful tool, especially for guarantors, will be the ability to share their information with schools, many of whom have a perfectly good address in their records; privacy concerns have previously prohibited the exchange of that information. The National Student Loan Data Base mandated in reauthorization certainly will identify those who are attempting to rip off the system through outright fraud and multiple loans, along with those who may not be attempting fraud but simply are in default and attempting to get another loan elsewhere.

While there are some questions concerning the cost of student loan consolidation within the Administration, consolidation does offer the possibility of helping individuals with true cash flow situations. The job is still large—the bathtub is still filling up faster than it's emptying, at least in the guaranteed loan program. Combining all sources, we will collect around a quarter of a billion in default recoveries this year; at the same time, we will lose another billion in defaults. We are, however, beginning to accelerate the rate of collection. There is a very good possibility that the two lines will cross in the next few years, particularly with the continued fine efforts by the guarantee agencies. We rely on the continued confidence of the American people and the Congress in the effective administration of this program by all concerned. Finally, we depend on the continued availability of student loan funds for the benefit of the people whom we serve, the students of the United States of America.

Chapter 4

THE DILEMMAS OF LOAN COUNSELING: A PRACTITIONER VIEWPOINT

Ann Coles, Janice Dorian, Theresa Orr, and
Sylvia Quarles Simmons

Introduction, by Sylvia Quarles Simmons

There is no doubt that the student loan program is, and will continue to be, an important part of students' lives. As we move toward the year 2000, we need to be mindful of the roles that national interests and state policies will play in determining who pays for higher education. Nor can we ignore the impacts of changing technology, unemployment, manpower needs, and demographics.

By 1992 half of all students in higher education will be part-time and over 25. By the year 2010, one in three will be black, Hispanic, or Asian-American. The residual responsibility for financing their education, if all else fails, will rest with them. Older students will not have parental resources, and they will not be able to earn a sufficient amount to finance full-time attendance. Accordingly, this new group of students will be likely to borrow as much as possible and to attend school part-time. Some will choose a short-term career/vocational school in order to obtain a marketable skill.

We must begin paying attention to the education of students we will have rather than to the students we would like to have. In terms of student loans, we must provide the counseling these borrowers will request. We have to broaden our ability to serve a diverse group and test our assumptions about the cultural aspects of borrowing through research. Only by working together can we gain a consensus from the participants who share the responsibility for financing higher education, define and gather the data (such as ability to pay, extent of borrowing, earning limits, and unmet need) needed to maintain a balance, define the needs of a changing student body, and monitor the external forces that will affect that balance.

In the perspective statements that follow, three practitioners stimulate this challenge by offering their concerns about student borrowing, observations about the special needs of certain categories of students, and, in particular, perceptions about the dilemmas of loan counseling.

Perspective: Theresa Orr, Director of Financial Aid, Harvard Medical School

An increasingly important area of focus for financial aid practitioners is effective student loan counseling. In its simplest terms, loan counseling is plain required disclosure—making sure the prospective borrower knows that the loan has to be paid back and on what terms and conditions. What the Massachusetts Higher Education Assistance Corporation Loan Counseling Task Force (referred to hereafter as the Task Force) describes as loan counseling is not a single event but rather the process of credit education. We conceive of it as taking place at multiple times during a student's pre-borrowing, borrowing, and repayment life and as covering a broad range of steps.

The question of who has the responsibility to counsel was entertained only briefly by the Task Force because it seemed apparent that all of us—schools, lenders, and guarantee agency—share that responsibility. No one entity bears the sole obligation to counsel. The loan counseling model developed by the Task Force involves everyone at different times in the process.

But the fact remains that, according to the recent NASFAA study on GSL repayers, the postsecondary schools are the best source of information for student borrowers. And the Senate reauthorization bill proposes to place into law the school's responsibility to provide loan counseling. So our Task Force was perhaps visionary in developing tools for the already burdened school administrators to carry out their expanded role. These materials include pamphlets, brochures, posters, workbooks, and audio-visual materials, and they of course engage the other groups of concern as well—the lenders and the guarantor.

The Task Force has met regularly since 1983 under the auspices of Massachusetts Higher Education Assistance Corporation. The group includes lenders, schools, community agencies, the high school, and the guarantee agency. Both lender representation and school representation are diverse.

As a task force we read all the available literature. We read studies that suggest certain ethnic, income, or psychological characteristics as a means to identify a potential student loan defaulter, but we found little empirical evidence to support any such generalizations. We concluded that there is no definitive profile of a defaulter; instead, we found that the single most frequent feature of importance was borrower attitude. We have come to describe the successful loan repayer as one who fully understands his/her financial obligations and who is willing to accept whatever lifestyle restrictions the loan obligation may impose. The NASFAA study reinforced our conclusion, finding that borrowers using 10 percent or more of income to repay student loans experience an impact on other lifestyle choices. But most borrowers repay because they are committed to doing so.

Having reached the conclusion that willingness to repay is even more important than ability to repay, the Task Force asked the question, "How can we influence the willingness of borrowers to repay student loans?" Our response was to determine that credit education and loan counseling must take place at multiple times and with different emphases during a student borrower's developmental life. The Task Force developed a comprehensive loan counseling model which involves the schools, the lenders, and the guarantor. Each of these groups has a share in the opportunity and obligation to counsel and is involved at different times. The model is an informational one which includes activities, materials, publications, and the training needed to provide information about the six areas we distilled from our reading and discussions: credit financing, alternatives to borrowing, the application process, how much to borrow, repayment, and consequences of default.

Our model assumes that we can begin education about loans early. Through this plan, we will reach youngsters initially as early as junior high school by presenting a basic understanding of what it means to use credit to buy things. At the high school level, we want students to know that higher education is possible for anyone and that loans are available to help pay for it. Loans, of course, are only one way to finance higher education. We want students to understand both the consequences of borrowing and the alternatives to borrowing. We want students who are already in higher education to make the most informed choice possible about how much to borrow, to understand the terms of each of their loans, and to be prepared for repayment. And we also want to be of service to those borrowers who have already left higher education and are bewildered by the loan repayment process. Our target groups, therefore, include: junior high and high school students, borrowers in school, borrowers in repayment, borrowers in default, and the general public.

Borrowers in repayment benefitted from our first completed project in March 1985, when we conducted our first Repayment Hotline for borrowers with education loans. Posters in the MBTA (the Boston area mass transit authority) generated most of the 800 calls. Besides requests for general information, most hotline callers wanted to know about consolidation, deferment, default, and forbearance. Our second repayment hotline took place during the month of October 1986 and will be reoffered annually.

The repayment target group was also the focus of our second project. The GSL repayment booklet, "Everything You Always Wanted to Know About Repaying Your GSL," was completed shortly after the hotline. Also for this group, MHEAC published a lender stuffer for use with accounts 60 days prior to the beginning of repayment called "Making the Most of Your Grace Period."

For the high school target group, in the spring of 1985 MHEAC conducted a logo art contest in the high schools of Massachusetts. Students were invited to design a logo for the Loan Counseling Task Force. Contest entrants had to be introduced to our basic loan counseling concepts. Governor Michael Dukakis presented a citation to the young winner, who also received a $500 scholarship from the Massachusetts Cooperative Bankers Association.

We also printed a pamphlet for high schools that opens as a poster and can be used at financial aid nights. Called "Be a Wise Borrower," it urges students to investigate all types of aid; to contemplate alternatives to borrowing; to evaluate financial aid packages; to calculate what a loan will mean to them after leaving school; and to dedicate themselves to repayment. And, we have an educational tool to be used by the guidance counselors called "Life with a Student Loan: A Play in Two Acts: Borrowing/Repayment."

For in-school borrowers as well as high-schoolers, we have developed two flipcharts: one on the 10 steps to applying for a GSL and the other on the 10 steps to repaying a GSL. The flipcharts can be produced as a slide show or video and have multiple uses. Major pieces directed to the in-school borrowers are an entrance/exit interview tool called "It's Your Choice . . ." and a workbook called "How Much Can I Afford to Borrow?" We also prepared a teacher lesson kit on the wise use of credit for the junior high school, a poster series, an exhibit for shopping malls and college fairs, and an audio-visual presentation incorporating our six loan counseling themes in the planning stages. And we continue to produce publicity items like T-shirts, stickers, bags, pens, and so forth to reinforce the message of the Task Force.

A critical concept that we believe all loan counseling must include is how debt relates to future income and lifestyle choices. This element is crucial to all of the target groups. Students can be helped to understand that their education is a valuable investment and that obtaining an education is worthwhile, even though they may have to rearrange future priorities.

Besides the major target groups there are certain categories of borrowers, such as adult borrowers and students who have withdrawn from school, who need special attention. Although the model is for the most part generic, we do not want to ignore groups with special needs. The message which underlies our program is that responsibility to avoid default rests with the borrower. But, all of our investigations support our understanding that students are usually inexperienced borrowers whose first form of credit is the student loan, and that we frequently make mistakes the first time we do something. The Task Force aims to help students become experienced repayers. In addition, our intent is to help student loan providers and school administrators respond to the dilemmas of loan counseling.

Perspective: Ann Coles, Director of Higher Education Information Center

The dilemmas that face adult and female borrowers are a special concern in loan counseling. These are difficult categories even to describe generally because there are so many different breeds. Some individuals are in undergraduate school or borrowing for graduate or professional school; some adults are resuming their education after being away from school, and some are starting higher education for the first time. Some adult borrowers are working full-time and going to school part-time.

The capacity of the adult borrower to handle loan responsibility also depends on a number of other factors such as a person's previous work experience and the level of income one can predict on the basis of that experience. Obviously, the more work experience a person has, the greater the income he or she will generate once working, unless a big career change is involved. The other financial responsibilities the adult borrower may have—such as mortgages and car payments—are factors. The career the person is planning to go into and the level of income to be expected in that career are important factors as well. And finally, prior experience with borrowing and the kind of confidence people have in their capacity to borrow—to juggle priorities, to figure out how to manage money, to manage repayments—must be considered.

One specific category of borrower is the adult female undergraduate borrower. First of all, whether married, divorced, or single, the majority of women in this category often have responsibilities for dependent children. The primary motivating factor for them to go to college or resume education is their desire to improve their job opportunities, make more money, and be better prepared to help support their families. In many instances these women are single parents; often, they are the sole support of their children or have limited child support to supplement what they can generate themselves.

Women have much more difficulty than their male counterparts in obtaining well-paying jobs. Women with four-year college degrees earn an average of 63 percent of what men with high school diplomas earn. And, there is about a 50 percent differential between the expected lifetime earnings of men and of women. The implications for women's capacity to handle loans are obvious.

Another factor to be considered is that adult women who have completed their undergraduate education, even though they have many more financial responsibilities than younger women just coming out of college, are still entry-level people in the labor market. That is to say, a 35-year-old woman with a bachelor's degree will begin at the same salary level as a 22-year-old woman. This is true even though the 35-year-old may have two children, higher rent, and many more expenses than the 22-year-old, as well as limited mobility in terms of being able to move to new places to work.

The female adult borrower must consider, even when she gets out of school, that she is already living close to the margin; she does not have a lot of flexibility. She may have heavy costs, and most of the money to which she has access may be needed to cover very basic expenses. Women comprise two-thirds of the borrowers who have to commit more than 10 percent of their income to student loans. Some studies have shown that of the borrowers who had to commit 10 percent of income, 80 percent were single, and many of those single borrowers had dependent children. It obviously is much more stressful to carry the responsibility of a loan with these responsibilities.

Despite the difficulties listed above, the borrower should assume primary responsibility for loan repayment. We need to be more aware, however, of how very hard it is for adults, particularly adults with limited borrowing experience, to know exactly where to go for information. Therefore, it is very important that lenders and schools provide such information. Schools are the first choice because adult borrowers with limited experience or limited resources are somewhat intimidated by bankers. Many people are afraid to ask too many questions for fear they will reveal something about themselves that will make it impossible for them to get the loan. Schools are an excellent source of such information. Not only are they readily accessible— the student is right there—but this process gives them another way to make education personalized.

It is important to emphasize that schools and banks should urge students to borrow only what they need to meet their educational costs. Too often in my work in community colleges in Massachusetts, I have seen low-income women view student loans as an opportunity to pay off utility bills or car loans, get something fixed, or do something for their kids. They know that these uses are not what the money is for, but they feel a bit desperate. For their part, lenders often see loans a bit differently from the way others see them. For instance, some lenders will not make loans for less than $1,000 because of the processing costs. If the student needs only $750, however, the most responsible and helpful thing a lender can do is to make a loan that does not substantially exceed the need.

Schools should emphasize the alternatives to borrowing and help students think of other ways they can manage besides borrowing. Before time comes for repayment, students will benefit from career counseling. They need to think early in their educational career about the kind of job they want after graduation. They can be preparing as freshmen, sophomores, and juniors for those kinds of jobs by participating in internships, coops, and work-study jobs as a way to build a reservoir of job experience that will help them get into the labor market. Obviously, there are potentially many different kinds of help. Ideally, the school will play a role by providing students with instruction in financial management and planning by experts—by people who have both some ideas and some solutions.

Some research reports indicate that borrower attitude is the single most important factor in terms of a student's likelihood of repayment—that is, willingness to repay. Two factors are involved: First, the student borrower must understand the obligations being assumed; second, he or she must be prepared to undertake lifestyle compromises. Certainly the women I have known who have borrowed money have been very willing to borrow. However, when it comes to understanding the obligation, many women lack basic information. Typically, they have not previously borrowed a lot; they do not understand borrowing and are reluctant to ask such questions as, "If I borrow $1,500 for the next four years, how much will I have to earn to pay it back?"

Much information about student loans is available at the typical college financial aid office, but the first thing the student sees is a big counter. The information is behind that counter somewhere, but there are real fears, such as: "They'll find out that I don't really know much." "They'll find out that I've never taken out a loan before." "They'll find out that I don't have a whole lot of credit." "They'll find out that my husband doesn't want me doing this, and I'm doing it pretty much on my own." Or, "They'll think

I'm a risky borrower, so I better not ask those questions."
So the need for information and the perceived risk in
getting it become a dilemma.

In the repayment stage, lifestyle adjustments and compromises are very important characteristics, but an adult
woman returning to school because she needs to be able to
earn more money may be quite limited in terms of making
lifestyle adjustments. She cannot take her children and
find a roommate with whom to share an apartment the way
a single person can. If she takes a second job at night, she
has to pay for a babysitter. She has a whole set of monthly
financial obligations that are fundamental parts of life—the
utilities, rent, telephone. In short, she is limited in her
capacity to make lifestyle adjustments even though that,
theoretically, is what needs to be done.

Although there is always a need for help with financial
management and career counseling, it is not always easy to
get this kind of help in institutions. I have evaluated the
congruence between student needs for counseling and
other kinds of support services on the one hand, and the
availability of such services on the other hand, in the
Boston area. The colleges there have many support services available and the students have many needs for them,
but students indicate that they do not use them to any
great extent. This is a problem for which the institution
must take responsibility. The ways in which these services
are organized at most postsecondary institutions make it
very difficult for them to deliver coherently the kind of
advice and assistance that people need. Financial aid officers are not career counselors, career counselors are not
student employment people, student employment people
are not internship coordinators, internship coordinators
are not co-op people, and co-op people are not job placement people. In short, the services are unorganized and
widely dispersed.

The concerns, for example, of the adult female borrower
are interlocking problems that require an integrated solution. Yet, most student affairs and financial aid people do
not interact much except over coffee and lunch; they fail to
see the overall problem. The fact that many of the students

involved are commuters with off-campus responsibilities adds to the problem; they simply do not have time to run around to several different offices. Subsequently, these students often do not make their needs known, and they do not receive the benefit of institutional resources.

This problem for adult and female students is also a problem for the schools. It is in the interest of postsecondary institutions to help students and to counsel them so that they will repay their loans conscientiously. After all, postsecondary institutions depend heavily on the availability of student loans for attendance. Responsible borrowing, moreover, is congruent with the lofty and admirable philosophy of many postsecondary institutions that people should be prepared for life in practical terms. Certainly it is important for everyone to know how to be financially responsible. By helping students understand the responsibility for repaying loans and by encouraging them to do so in a conscientious way, educators can perform a real and lasting service.

Perspective: Janice Dorian, Financial Aid Director, Mansfield Beauty School

There are three types of one-time student borrowers, the first of which is the student who attends an institution offering a one-year program. (These programs are primarily in proprietary institutions.) The second is a student who attends any institution for two or four years, and the third is a student who attends any institution for a time but who terminates from school.

Wilford Wilms, writing for the National Commission on Student Financial Assistance, reports that some of the general characteristics of the one-time borrower are as follows: 82 percent are female and 18 percent are male; 48 percent are white, 32 percent are black, and 18 percent Hispanic; 52 percent have family incomes of less than $7,000; 39 percent are dependent and 61 percent are independent; 36 percent are under the age of 20, 51 percent are between 20 and 35, and 13 percent are over 35.

The majority of students attending proprietary institutions are from economically disadvantaged backgrounds. Fifty percent of their federal aid resources come from loans, primarily because of the diminishing number of grant programs. Proprietary institutions participate only marginally in the campus-based programs.

Counseling for one-time borrowers has to take a different perspective. The average loan for these borrowers will go into repayment anywhere from seven to sixteen months after than loan is issued—a quick turnaround time. The maximum loan is approximately $2,500. These students can be encouraged to pay off their loan or a portion of it during the grace period. Doing so will not only reduce interest payments over the lifetime of the loan but also help to promote a proper attitude toward borrowing and repayment.

The majority of these borrowers attend an institution near home. They work, attend school, and bank in the same area. It is important for them not only to establish good credit but also to establish a good working relationship with their lender. These students, after all, hope to return to the lender within a one- to five-year period for a car loan, a home loan, or, as in the case of many beauty school graduates, a business loan. If these borrowers are nurtured properly, they will be able to develop a good credit history and will be life-long customers of the lender.

GSLs are targeted primarily for lower-income students unable to attend the postsecondary institution of their choice without aid. Yet these are primarily the most disadvantaged of all students and those who will have the greatest difficulty repaying. Wilms' study also shows that these students need more access to grant programs in order to reduce their dependency on loans.

Regarding repayment, I like to think of it as a wheel of responsibility, where the different spokes of the wheel are made up of the student, the lender, the guarantee agency, and the educational institution. In order for this wheel to rotate properly, each party must bear his or her share of the weight. It is important for students to recognize that loan money comes from lenders—lenders must be first to stress this. It is also important for schools to accept the responsibility attendant to being in touch with the students for the longest period of time and, therefore, having the best opportunity to counsel and inform them.

The essential points on which we have to educate the students are threefold. They have to know: (1) that they have received a loan, not a gift, (2) that it needs to be repaid, and (3) that they are still responsible for repaying the loan even if the program for which the loan was made is not completed, or even if they do not receive a job in the area for which they were trained. They must understand that the education they receive, whether it is a partial or a complete package, is an asset, and that every asset has value. If one borrows to obtain this asset, one must repay that loan. It is important, in this connection, that there be counseling on careers and the impact of the total loan burden. Students have to understand that the kind of career they want may determine whether or not they will be able to pay off their loans. And they have to understand that there are consequences for not repaying.

One issue of great concern is how to ensure that all the participants in student assistance programs—federal government, lenders, schools, guarantors—coordinate their philosophies. For example, a proprietary institution normally spends time counseling the student to borrow only what is needed. If that student is told by the lending institution, for example, that he or she must borrow a minimum of a thousand dollars when only $700 is needed, or if a student's loan is increased to $2,500 automatically regardless of need and without the school even knowing about it, serious problems can ensue. In fairness to the lending community, however, it is important for educators to create incentives for small loan amounts, for in reality it is expensive to process and collect a small package.

A final matter for consideration is the cost of counseling students. It is not enough simply to produce informative pamphlets, charts, and videotapes; these information tools must be properly used. If schools are to do this job properly, they must have adequate staff. Hiring more staff, of course, increases institutional expenses, and that often leads to increased tuition. In this regard, we should consider what the increased dependency on loans as well as other financial aid dollars is doing to the cash-paying students—the students who are not eligible to receive financial aid. Is it tending to eliminate them? From an institutional perspective, costs that do not add to the education being offered or provide additional student services put the school in a very tenuous situation. Mandating student loan counseling and placing sole responsibility for it on the schools may well be counterproductive in that the cost to the federal government and to students will be too high.

Ultimately the student is responsible for repayment. Although student profiles vary from school to school, according to Dr. Jerry Davis of the Pennsylvania Higher Education Assistance Agency, institutional variations in default rates are more closely related to the characteristics of borrowers who attend school than to the characteristics, policies, and practices of schools themselves. Proprietary institutions, for example, have a large percentage of disadvantaged students, and this fact ultimately will be reflected in their default rate.

In conclusion, it is essential that lending institutions, government and its agencies, guarantee agencies, and schools cooperate to eliminate as many reasons for defaulting as possible. It is not sufficient simply to give students tougher regulations. Rather, we must use our collective wisdom and resources to make it easier for students both to obtain the type of education they want and to repay the loans they undertake to finance it.

Section Two

THE IMPACT OF
STUDENT
LOANS ON ACCESS

Does the existing financial aid system adequately serve the needs of all age groups, all races, all categories of the citizenry who could benefit from postsecondary education? One set of voices during the 1980s advocate the reduction of federal financial aid. Some say, "Let them work their way through school the way we did." Others say parents should pay all or most of the costs. Another viewpoint expressed by the U.S. Secretary of Education calls for almost exclusive reliance on loans, even to $10,000 a year for undergraduate students who would then repay their loans over a working lifetime.

Another set of voices wonders why the nation does not offer full tuition scholarships, or waive tuition and fees, for the economically disadvantaged students of all races. In the 1970s the Carnegie Foundation suggested a compromise: that every graduate from high school receive two years of postsecondary education free of charge, usable at any point in his or her lifetime. These "two years in the bank" exist in some states such as California for community colleges, as they did for many years (until 1975) in the City University of New York.

The most eloquent advocate for women, minorities, and the economically disadvantaged with unmet needs is Dr. Dolores Cross of the New York State Higher Education Services Corporation. Her agency has surveyed the unmet needs of New York

State, one of the nation's best organized systems of providing for postsecondary education. She employs 800 persons to administer $1 billion a year of education loans and $460 million of state scholarship tuition grants, an amount roughly equivalent to the federal Pell grant program for New York State. She describes the unmet needs of underserved and inadequately financed individuals in New York State.

Simultaneously, the New England Board of Higher Education completed a survey of enrollment by minorities in colleges in the six New England states. Many policymakers and higher education officials report a decline in the attendance of minorities and want a thorough documentation of minorities in New England colleges.

The issues remain very complex. Responsible economists, educators, and businessmen suggest that the use of loans for at least a portion of higher education is defensible. But there remain severe problems in relying on education loans for part-time students, especially those who need six to eight years to complete a baccalaureate degree. Grants and scholarships may be more cost-effective mechanisms to finance at least the first half of their education. The "solution" of making all federal financial aid programs including loans available for part-time adult learners, especially those on AFDC or public welfare rolls, may be a disservice. Certain populations are especially vulnerable and may need insulation from indebtedness for the initial years of postsecondary education. Stated most positively, grants may be more appropriate for the first two or four semesters of college for "high risk" students, with loans coming later. Lenders find it difficult to make loans that will not be repaid for many years. Deferring interest payments and accruing and capitalizing those amounts over a four- to eight-year period can be excessively expensive to the borrower.

The next step is to examine carefully the demographic characteristics and educational needs of low-income youth and adults, of minorities and women. Then we must fashion the financial strategies that respond to those needs. The next two selections address those issues. A uniquely Boston response, the ACCESS program, is described in an appendix to this volume. ACCESS, which serves the inner-city youth who graduate from the Boston public high schools, is but one strategy for the 1990s.

Chapter 5

ACCESS TO HIGHER EDUCATION: A SHARED RESPONSIBILITY

Dolores E. Cross

Chancellor Clifton Wharton, speaking to the National Urban League in San Francisco, created a useful frame of reference for an inquiry into the education of urban youth, minorities, and women in terms of access to higher education:

> *Today's appalling school dropout and stalling of progress in higher education are two aspects of what I believe to be an impending education crisis for black Americans. It is a crisis that may be transformed all too soon into an outright disaster. Must it be that we will have to light our own way? If so, let our light be the lamp of learning, and let it burn brighter today than yesterday and burn brighter tomorrow than today.*

There is no question but that education provides a better quality of life for its participants. But there are, obviously, pressing concerns about educational opportunities. We need to think more about some basic questions, such as: Whatever happened to our concern for equity? Whatever happened to our passion for equality? Is the job done, or is there more to do?

In the context of these concerns, a retrospective and prospective look at the financial aid story will help us focus

on the situation today. We need to consider all of the
following: federal financial aid developments since the
1960s; warning signs over the past five years that a crisis in
access exists; and necessary actions to improve our respon-
siveness to minorities, older women, and other non-traditional students. Hopefully, reviewing this information will,
at the very least, direct our efforts toward reversing the
trend of declining minority enrollments in higher education.

The Development of a Crisis

In the early 1960s, civil rights legislation increased large-
scale aid to education. The Higher Education Act of 1965
embodied an explicit federal commitment equalizing college opportunities for needy students through educational
opportunity grants, college work-study, and outward
bound programs. Appropriations for student aid grew
while other forms of federal support gradually faded. By
1972 federal legislation for Pell grants, the SSIG (state
supplemental incentive grant), and state agencies for GSLs
increased. This battery of federal programs in place by the
mid-1970s were designed to equalize opportunities and,
through the Middle Income Student Assistance Act, get
dollars to the middle-income groups.

President Carter expanded these programs through the
Education Amendments of 1980. Then, in 1981, the
Reagan Administration launched a campaign to increase
dollars for defense and to drastically reduce dollars for
social programs, including higher education. It is fair to say
that for many people—many black Americans, many poor
people—Ronald Reagan's election to the presidency of the
United States was the first sign of a threat to access to
postsecondary education for eligible students.

The Reagan Administration years since have been
fraught with warning signs of a crisis in higher education
that may be transformed all too soon into outright disaster.
The Administration withdrew Social Security education
benefits, and its policy of level funding of federal student

aid programs has resulted in a real dollar loss of up to 20 percent in the Title IV student aid programs. Another warning sign was the Administration's aggressive promotion of proposals calling for drastic cutbacks in federal student aid. Although the result may not have been substantially fewer dollars, many students were discouraged by what they read in the headlines and felt that there was little hope.

The NYSHESC recently completed a random sample study of 8,000 New York students. In 1981–1982, with data on both recipients and non-recipients of aid, the study documented increased borrowing by low-income students and the full-time employment of full-time low-income students. At the same time we called attention to minority students' perception of financial aid as critical to their ability to be in school. The warning signs were there, with attending evidence that clearly showed an erosion of federal student assistance. Yet, for many policymakers the jury is still out on the issue of student hardships and on its impact on declines in minority enrollment. Our comments from students, families, and financial aid officers demonstrate that the evidence is already conclusive.

What has happened since 1981? The Administration's actions triggered a subtle change in attitude as well as shifts in the student aid packages. First, as the President threatened to withdraw or reduce aid dollars, many colleges began to move access down on the priority list and to talk less about need-based aid and more about merit-based aid. Poor, low-income students were left to languish, drop out, or change their plans. Second, relatively little attention was given to changes in the financial aid package that were not appropriate for low-income students—for example, increased borrowing. Consider that in 1975–1976, grant dollars made up 80 percent of the student's aid package; by 1984, grant dollars made up only approximately 47 percent of the aid package, with a correspondingly large increase in GSL borrowing by low-income students. Third—and this may be the most important factor—observations by financial aid administrators and surveys by state agencies documented the fact that the hardships students were experi-

encing did little to change prevailing attitudes about the
financial strength of many families and students.

At the City University of New York, for example, the
head count has remained pretty much the same, but there
has been a noticeable shift from full-time to part-time.
Many students have had to change their plans: Some are
going to school part-time of necessity; some have had to
drop out, some have had to stop temporarily. These are
low-income students, the non-traditional students. They
are the very students who triggered the development of
the financial aid policy in the first place. We are seeing
what could have been predicted from the 1980 early
warning signs mentioned above.

Looking to the Future

What do we do now? First, we must avoid doom and
gloom. It will be more productive to state the realities of
the situation and to look ahead in terms of what we need to
know so that we can, in Chancellor Wharton's words, "light
the way and continue with the lamp of learning." There is
every indication that we must immediately initiate steps to
re-examine our student financial aid policies, whose effectiveness is being affected by the growing number of non-
traditional students.

There will be new groups of people in postsecondary
education. These people will be Americans, some of whom
have been victims of oppressive traditions in the past.
English will not be the native language to some, and others
will come from diverse cultures and be at a lower socioeconomic level. This nation will soon include 44 million
blacks, 47 million Hispanics, and at least 10 million Asian-
Americans. All in all, there will be approximately 100
million minority persons in a nation of 260 million by about
2020. That means that one out of every three Americans
will be non-white.

At the same time, a greater percentage of minorities will
have relatively low incomes because of several factors.
First, a higher percentage of minority children come from

single-parent, female-headed households. Second, although the number of high school graduates among blacks and Hispanics has risen, college enrollments have been declining from the 1980 levels. Reasons for the drop include uncertainty about student aid and a reduction in counseling and other support activities for minority students. Efforts must be made to learn more about these students—more about them in terms of multi-cultural education, of their expectations and values concerning education, and of the supports they need.

The non-traditional student has become a focus of interest as the demographics of the college-going population shift. Some schools are scrambling for enrollments, and the women's movement has raised the level of awareness about problems faced by those who have been treated as second-class citizens. We acknowledge that non-traditional students and institutions of higher education need each other and that a strong market during the next decade will be the adult learner who is probably a head of household, probably a woman or a minority, or both. It is estimated that by 1992 half of all college students will be over 25, and that 20 percent will be over 35. Where are the programs to support these changes?

Additionally, the nature of the American family is shifting in ways that directly affect the youth and adults who will be entering higher education in the next decade. The "traditional" family comprises only 11 percent of households in the United States today. Changes in family structure have triggered the return of many adult women to college campuses. Since 1972 the number of women over the age of 25 enrolled in college has more than doubled. Data from the National Center for Education Statistics indicate that by 1988 approximately 2.5 million adult women will be enrolled in some form of education. However, these women are over-represented in community colleges and vocational programs and are under-represented in professional programs, especially those leading to higher-paying employment.

A review of some data presented at a series of New York State hearings on the feminization of poverty in 1984 shows why non-traditional student women feel that they need to attend college. First, women are clustered in low-paid occupations such as clerical and service workers. Nationally, only 13 percent of all female heads of household worked in professional or technical positions. More than a third of all female-headed families are living below the poverty threshold defined by the federal government—36 percent nationally and 34 percent in New York State. Nationally, between 70 and 80 percent of families headed by minority women are living in poverty. At the state level, 40 percent of black female-headed households and 60 percent of Hispanic female-headed households are below the poverty level.

Higher education does represent a way for women and minorities to break the cycle of poverty, but even college-educated women face structural barriers to advancement. A wide range of educational options is necessary for women entering or returning to the workforce. Two-year degree programs are necessary. Advanced, but focused, further education for women with bachelors degrees is necessary. Short-term vocational and skills training and further training to promote career mobility—especially in view of the changing structure of the economy and job market—are necessary.

Life-long learning is a fact of life today for about half the American adult population. Colleges and universities are a part of this picture, but many workers are taking courses offered in the workplace and getting the benefit of the educational programs of companies, corporations, and even state government. Still many barriers to educational access exist for older and returning students. They are faced not only with financial problems but also with lack of information, transportation difficulties, need for receptive counseling, and problems with safety and security.

An increase in the proportion of non-traditional students also means that educational institutions will increasingly have to deal with questions involving the interaction between student financial aid and other major benefit programs. Unclear policies concerning such interaction can create barriers to the use of educational programs by older and returning students, particularly women. Recipients of public assistance programs may face additional hardships through grant cuts or termination if they seek full-time education other than training through a job-training partnership. If someone is receiving financial aid and is also on welfare, treatment varies depending upon the income maintenance center involved. Some income maintenance centers will cut back payments, taking the position that a person on welfare should live like it—that is, not on a student budget, but on a welfare budget. For people on welfare seeking to go to school, there is often a real problem of harassment and pressure, and they feel the impact of contradictory state and federal policies. Students who are receiving aid can even have their food stamp eligibility affected.

For non-English speaking students, instruction in the English language and remedial instruction may not qualify for aid. Other problems such as poor academic preparation, lag time since their last educational experience, scheduling conflicts, and lack of family support interact with one another and have cumulative negative effects on the educational experience of older and returning students. Higher education institutions and programs are finding it increasingly necessary to become more flexible in order to accommodate the needs of older students—necessary for both moral and economic reasons. In New York State there are more than 650 postsecondary institutions which enroll more than a million students. These institutions of postsecondary education contribute at least $7 billion annually to New York State's economy and employ over 200,000 faculty and staff.

It would appear to be good business sense to protect the investment that we have in our educational establishment by exploring ways to improve the enrollment and retention of a growing population segment. College administrators have already realized that non-traditional students may provide the revenue they need. They have expanded their recruitment drives into shopping malls and even into homes and businesses via direct mailings and attractive course listings. As the proportion of older, part-time stu-

dents increases, schools need to rethink their class scheduling and provision of support services in order to reflect
these students' needs. Such reforms could include, first,
extended hours for registrar, bursar, admissions, and advisory offices. In many cases these offices close at 5:00 P.M.
and students do not have access to the information they
need. Second, information centers and child-care centers
for day and evening could be established. Third, support
service offices could be clustered in one central location so
that the student does not have to go all over the campus to
get information.

The changing composition of the student body also
means that we need to restructure the traditional expectation of earning a college degree in four years. Many older
and returning students and non-traditional students will
need more than four years to complete their degrees
because of economic necessity, family responsibility, and
also the difficulties attendant to becoming a student after
being out of school for a while.

When policymakers discuss the demographic projections
for the year 2000, there must be more attention paid to the
student financial aid policy that will be necessary then.
Our policymakers must heed the signs. We cannot allow
what has happened since 1970—and what put us to where
we are today—to continue. Financial aid facilitates access
to education and training. It provides a critical link between the economic backgrounds of non-traditional students and their higher education aspirations. But appropriate methods need to be developed, methods that
realistically measure the discretionary income that non-
traditional students have available.

How does one compute the financial need of a 40-year-
old mother raising two children without support from their
father? Many campuses are already dealing with the complexities of constructing expense budgets, conducting
needs analysis, and designing consistent financial award
policies for largely non-traditional student bodies. Students who are older often attend less than full-time and
typically are coping with work and family roles. In addition, most federal and state student aid programs do not

allow a person to take six years or more to complete a degree, even though many people cannot possibly complete their degrees in four years.

The importance of financial aid counseling to non-traditional students must not be underestimated. A greater knowledge of financial aid programs, eligibility requirements, application delivery procedures, and appropriate loan amounts provide a foundation that is essential for these students. Financial aid people must be sensitive to the special needs of non-traditional students, especially women, minorities, groups who have been traditionally underserved, and groups whose parents have been the victims of oppressive traditions such as racism and sexism in this country.

It is important that financial aid personnel expand their efforts and become as creative as possible. One way is to begin disseminating information beyond the traditional places such as pre-college guidance centers at the community level. New York has identified 2,000 community organizations in the state to which we send information on available programs and promotional brochures that say, "You can afford college." Our hope is that this information will be helpful to parents and students as they work together and think things through. Each of us should identify new outlets for information.

We also need to be sure that the information we develop will catch students' attention. I recently suggested to a group of young people at Vassar (who were talking about minority recruitment) that they develop a rap song. Students, as we know, can remember all the words to a rap song. That is an example of using a non-traditional approach to get the message to a non-traditional student.

Part-time students may, indeed, become the norm in the not-too-distant future. Financial aid programs that address their needs and recognize that some of these students may have to "stop out" periodically are critical. Some of these "stop-outs" may have defaulted on their student loans. They need to know that in New York, for example, eligibility can be reinstated for regularly repaying defaulters. Students also need to be made more aware of new, more comprehensive verification requirements so that when they apply for aid, they will have the appropriate documentation.

In 1984 Governor Cuomo of New York proposed for the first time a student financial aid program to assist students who attend postsecondary institutions at least half, but less than full, time. The program was a major step in recognizing the growing number of New Yorkers who must attend college on a part-time basis. Up to $2,000 a year in tuition aid is available to these part-time students, with awards based on the student's need and tuition cost determined by the educational institution. This program benefits low-income, part-time students who predominantly fit into the non-traditional student mold. The significance of this assistance for part-time study in relation to women and minorities cannot be overlooked; it is a signal that New York State's leadership, at least, recognizes the problems and is taking steps toward a solution. Of equal importance is the generational impact of such assistance. Children, especially daughters, are observing their mothers as role models, and they are learning that higher education is also their prerogative. New York also has a tuition assistance enrichment program, providing $460 million in grants and scholarships to students—one-third of the grant dollars provided nationwide by states.

Economic realities necessitate the creation of alternative ways to provide student financial assistance. The substantial rises in college costs clearly are not being responded to with parallel increases in federal aid. Students who attend school full time are finding it increasingly necessary to work more hours in order to pay their education bills. Unfortunately, the attempt to be a full-time employee and a full-time student simultaneously is likely to have a negative impact on academic achievement. Some alternatives to student indebtedness that should be considered include:

- Fostering wider use of cooperative education.
- Creating summer and term-type jobs that pay well.
- Bringing down tuition costs.
- Creating public service jobs.

- Sponsoring stop-out programs which allow students to earn.
- Encouraging earlier parental savings.

State student financial aid agencies are playing an increasingly significant role in expanding educational access and in fostering choice. The 1985–1986 annual survey of the National Association of State Scholarship and Grant Programs indicated that state-funded grants and scholarships totaled $1.5 billion in 1985–1986, up 7 percent from the previous year. In New York, more than $460 million in state grants and awards will be expended in 1987.

Postsecondary institutions are developing new aid programs and seeking other sources of money to compensate for the shrinking of federal dollars. The range of institutional and private sector assistance can include tuition adjustment strategies, endowment funds, private student and parent loan programs, and cash-flow adjustments. Colleges also can make greater use of cooperative and work-study programs and provide more assistance to companies as they develop vocational training programs. An example of industry/college cooperation is found in the Corporate Education Exchange, a project of Boston's Council for Northeast Economic Action. The Exchange asks colleges to list programs that would interest businesses. When a business is in need of a training or specialized instruction program, the exchange alerts colleges with applicable programs. Various cooperative education programs enable students to pay a large percentage of tuition costs. Students alternate schedules between classes and off-campus work experience. Beyond financial benefits, co-op education offers students an opportunity to gain on-the-job experience.

Fortunately, the 1980s are beginning to see a growth of corporate interest and influence in education. Corporate leaders perceive education as an investment, and they are willing to form partnerships to share the responsibility of student aid and to pool resources for the development of human capital. They see quality education as necessary for individual growth and for economic development. Additionally, postsecondary institutions are willing to establish partnerships with business in order that students receive an education which matches the present and future needs of the workforce.

A Matter of Equity

How much progress has been made in providing equal access to education? How, indeed, do you measure progress? As an example, consider the experience of my daughter, a lawyer practicing in a New York City law firm. She recently said to me, "You really don't know how difficult it is for me. I know you feel very good about my working in this firm—but I'm the only black there." And she said this with a lot of pain. I replied to her, "Jane, you don't realize how difficult it is for me at 50 years old to sit across the table from you—you who are half my age—and hear you tell me that you're the only black in your firm." I am left with the question, "Whatever happened to equity?"

It seems fair to ask whether Americans are as responsive as we think we are. Have we really addressed the inequities of the past, including the crime of slavery and racism and other oppressive traditions? Are we developing a class-based society? Do we delude ourselves by saying that all of us can pull ourselves up by our own bootstraps rather than acknowledging the fact that many families are undercapitalized and do not have the dollars to meet the expected family contribution. Many people are afraid of loans, yet they have to borrow. They need guidance in money management and career planning in order to meet their indebtedness.

Escalating college costs are contributing direct pressures on students and their families as career paths are chosen and as factors related to enrollment and retention are considered. At the same time, policy recommendations at the federal levels could totally destroy the hopes and aspirations of students and families. We all will be affected by a loss of access, choice, and equity, whether through family attendance, institutional closure, or the disillusionment that is arising among youth faced with the denial of the educational opportunity. But the changes resulting from federal contraction of aid reach beyond postsecondary education. The Administration's moves to cut student aid represent a major step in reversing past gains that have been made in realizing our nation's fundamental goal of providing access, choice, and equity to its citizenry.

The students of this nation have a right to expect high-quality, responsive education. Educational and work opportunities are necessary in order that students in all groups be able to realize their potential and improve the quality of their lives. The fact that we recognize and value our ethnically pluralistic student population must be reflected in the total educational environments we provide. Policymakers must continue to emphasize and support quality in education. It is essential that we create academic and fiscal incentives that will attract students to teaching careers. At all governmental levels we need policy decisions which are sensitive to the needs of low-income, female, and minority students, in order to facilitate their access to our postsecondary education programs and our workforce.

Education can and must make a positive difference in the development of our society and in the quality of life of its citizens. Only through an unwavering commitment of student aid dollars for higher education can we ensure that the futures of students are not limited by stereotyping, segregation, or discrimination. I have no illusions that there will be more money from the federal government. Given the cutbacks and other problems in New York, it seems unlikely that there will be more dollars for grant programs. There is reason to hope, however, that people in higher education and concerned citizens will work with students to help them realize their aspirations. We should consider a mixture of full- and part-time study, but this solution will generate more than a few challenges. For example, how do you deal with institutions that provide a second-class program for part-time students? How do you help students who have defaulted on a student loan get back into the system, when through no fault of their own, they have not been able to get jobs?

In summary, our task, as we take a prospective look, is to use our interpersonal force—what we know about people—to help students gain access to the system and to refer to the realities around us to enhance sensitivity of policy-makers and refute the myth that the neediest are having all their financial aid needs met. This is not only the story about the non-traditional student, it is our story. And it is a story that must be considered as we look toward the year 2000.

Chapter 6

MINORITY STUDENTS IN HIGHER EDUCATION: A NEW ENGLAND PERSPECTIVE

Richard G. King

New England, particularly northern New England, has a relatively small minority population. With 5.3 percent of the nation's total population, New England has only 1.8 percent of U.S. blacks and 2 percent of its Hispanics. New England's three northern states collectively are home to less than 0.1 percent of either minority population. Yet these totals, while small relative to the rest of the country, are of substantial significance within the region: 475,000 New Englanders, 3.8 percent of the region's total population, are black, and 299,000, or 2.4 percent of the region's total, are Hispanic. In an era of labor shortages in the region, it is important that these groups have adequate access to the region's colleges and universities—but has New England been providing adequate access?*

Compared with the rest of the country, New England

---

*Note: This study does not examine the enrollment distribution of Native Americans because there are relatively few of them: 0.2 percent of the region's population, and 0.2 percent of college enrollments. Nor does it examine enrollment distributions of Asians, who apparently have been reasonably successful in gaining access to college; they represent 0.6 percent of the population of New England, but 1.6 percent of college enrollment in the region.

may appear to have been doing at least its share in enrolling minority students. With 1.8 percent of the nation's
blacks, New England has 2.5 percent of all black enrollments in higher education; and with 2 percent of the
nation's Hispanics, it has 2.5 percent of the nation's postsecondary Hispanic enrollments. Furthermore, those percentages of minority enrollments have been increasing
slightly but steadily since 1976, while national figures have
recently begun to decline. New England also has enrolled
more than its share of "non-resident aliens," or foreign
students.

But if one looks at the enrollment of minority students—
blacks, for example—in relation to total enrollments, the
record is less impressive. In 1984 in the nation as a whole,
11.7 percent of the total population but only 8.5 percent of
college students, were black. In New England 3.8 percent
of residents were black, but only 3.2 percent of college
enrollments were so reported. Among the New England
states, Connecticut had the highest percentage (7 percent)
of blacks in its total state population but only 4.4 percent in
its colleges, a figure that nevertheless led those of the
other New England states.

Connecticut's performance looks even better when one
compares public versus independent enrollments. Next to
Maine, Connecticut has the highest proportion (62.4 percent) of students enrolled in public institutions. When one
looks at minority enrollments, however, the proportion
enrolled in public institutions is even greater: 72.1 percent
for blacks and 69 percent for Hispanics. Massachusetts
public colleges, by contrast, with 43.7 percent of the state's
total enrollments, have only 38.4 percent of the state's
black enrollments in higher education and only 40.2 percent of the Hispanic. Connecticut's public colleges, in
other words, seem to be doing more than their share and
Massachusetts public colleges less. Connecticut and Massachusetts, incidentally, together have 92 percent of the
region's black population and 89 percent of the Hispanic.
The two states together boast 87 percent of the region's
black enrollments and an equal percentage of the region's
Hispanic enrollments.

State level statistics are important for general policy purposes, but they do not always elucidate complex issues well. Such is the case here. According to the 1980 census, the black and Hispanic populations of New England are concentrated in five major urban areas: Boston, Springfield, Hartford, New Haven, and Bridgeport. These five cities together house 56 percent of the region's total black population and 38 percent of the region's Hispanics.

Enrollment patterns dramatically parallel residential patterns. Financially pressed minority students often decide to commute to college, for obvious reasons. They are, by and large, enrolled in public community colleges (in the case of Connecticut) or in independent junior colleges or independent four-year colleges with special programs in business, music, or religion and to a much lesser extent in technology (in the case of Massachusetts). A few of the "Big Ivy," "Little Ivy," and "Seven Sister" colleges appear on the list; these are all institutions that recruit students nationally. At one "Big Ivy" college enrolling substantial numbers of minorities, only 13 percent of enrolled blacks and 4 percent of enrolled Hispanics came from the institution's home state. These colleges are making an important contribution but one that is more national than local or regional in scope and impact. Among the 42 colleges and universities in New England with 5 percent or more black enrollments, only one is a public four-year state college or state university (the University of Massachusetts at Boston).

It appears that while public and independent junior colleges and various specialized four-year institutions are opening their doors relatively wide to local minorities, older-line, more selective liberal arts or comprehensive institutions, public and independent, are not doing so well. A few urban institutions, such as Northeastern University, are notable exceptions.

The junior colleges, public and independent, are clearly providing a tremendously important public service. But in the absence of good information on retention, transfer, and ultimate graduation from four-year colleges—not to mention subsequent job histories—one can only conclude that minorities are not being given an equal chance of entering the traditional professions.

The problem of qualification for access, of course, begins in secondary school and even before—in elementary school, in the community, and in the home. Teachers and school administrators are obviously aware of all this, and even corporations recognize the need for early training, stimulation, and encouragement; witness the "Tri-Lateral" program, the Massachusetts Pre-engineering Program for Minority Students (Mass. PEP) in the Boston area, and Boston's new corporate-sponsored initiative, ACCESS, the Action Center for Educational Services and Scholarships.

Financial aid looms particularly large for minority students and their families. Constraints on direct aid and emphasis on loans in federal programs in the last few years have made many prospective applicants wary. This is especially true for blacks, a disproportionate number of whom come from single-parent families and see little prospect of freeing themselves from substantial indebtedness after graduation. Put positively, it is the enlightened federal, state, and institutional financial aid programs that helped produce the national growth in minority enrollment in the 1970s and early 1980s. To the extent that the federal government may now abdicate its supporting role, states and institutions must try even harder.

In summary, New England has a small proportion of black and Hispanic residents compared with the rest of the country, the corresponding national percentages being 11.7 percent for blacks and 6.4 percent for Hispanics. Nevertheless, these two groups in New England amount to over 700,000 individuals, a total of importance to a region with a labor shortage and a rapidly declining annual production of high school graduates. And yet only about 4.8 percent of the region's enrollments in higher education are black and Hispanic. Great efforts have been and are being made by effective, dedicated people, and the results show it. But for New England's liberal arts colleges and comprehensive universities, there are, as Robert Frost once wrote, "miles to go before we sleep."

Table 6-1   New England Cities with Concentrations of Blacks and
            Hispanics (1980)

City	Population	Black	Hispanic
Boston, Massachusetts	563,000	22.4%	6.4%
Springfield, Massachusetts	152,000	16.6%	9.1%
Bridgeport, Connecticut	143,000	21.0%	18.7%
Hartford, Connecticut	136,000	33.9%	20.5%
New Haven, Connecticut	126,000	31.9%	8.0%

Table 6-2   Unemployment Rates for Males and Females Ages 25 to 34

Race	1–3 Years High School	High School Graduates	2 Years College	4 Years College
White	15.4	7.7	3.6	2.6
Hispanic	15.1	10.3	4.4	2.9
Black	21.1	17.6	13.0	6.2

Table 6-3   Black Enrollment as a Percentage of Total Full-Time
            Enrollment

	1972	1976	1978	1980	1982	1984	Blacks as a Percentage of Total Population in Each State or Region
United States	8	9.4	9.4	9.1	8.9	8.5	11.7
New England	4	3.4	3.5	3.4	3.2	3.2	3.8
Connecticut	5	4.7	4.9	4.9	4.5	4.4	7.0
Massachusetts	4	3.7	3.7	3.5	3.4	3.5	3.9
Rhode Island	3	3.3	3.1	3.3	2.7	2.9	3.0
Maine	1	.6	.4	.4	.5	.5	.3
New Hampshire	2	1.4	1.5	1.6	1.4	1.2	.4
Vermont	2	1.4	1.1	1.0	.8	.7	.2

SOURCE: Center for Statistics, U.S. Office of Educational Research and Improvement.
From Statistical Abstract of the United States, 1986 NEBHE Analysis, July 1986.

Table 6-4   Colleges with 5 Percent or More Black Enrollment in 1984

CONNECTICUT

(P)	Greater Hartford Community College	27.3%
(P)	South Central Community College	22.1%
(P)	Norwalk Community College	15.4%
(I)	Hartford College for Women	14.2%
(P)	Housatonic Regional College	13.7%
(I)	Hartford Seminary	10.0%
(P)	Norwalk State Technical College	9.2%
(I)	Albertus Magnus College	7.3%
(I)	Wesleyan University	6.6%
(P)	Hartford State Technical College	5.5%
(I)	Yale University	5.0%

MASSACHUSETTS

(P)	Roxbury Community College	45.8%
(I)	Cambridge College/Institute of Open Education	23.2%
(I)	Atlantic Union College	21.8%
(I)	Newbury Junior College–Boston	19.2%
(I)	Bay State Junior College	13.5%
(I)	American International College	11.2%
(I)	Gordon-Conwell Theological Seminary	10.9%
(I)	Laboure College	10.7%
(P)	Bunker Hill Community College	10.1%
(P)	University of Massachusetts/Boston	9.8%
(I)	Amherst College	8.4%
(I)	Berklee College of Music	8.3%
(I)	Franklin Institute of Boston	8.2%
(I)	Chamberlayne Junior College	7.6%
(I)	Harvard/Radcliffe College (Harvard 4.2%)	6.9%
(P)	Springfield Tech. Community College	6.9%
(I)	Berkshire Christian College	6.3%
(I)	Swain School of Design	6.0%
(I)	Springfield College	6.0%
(I)	Boston Conservatory	6.0%
(I)	Hellenic College	5.9%
(I)	Massachusetts College of Pharmacy	5.6%
(I)	Wentworth Institute	5.5%
(I)	Northeastern University	5.5%
(I)	Wellesley College	5.4%
(I)	New England Institute of Applied Arts & Sciences	5.2%
(I)	Mt. Holyoke College	5.1%
(I)	Williams College	5.0%

RHODE ISLAND

(I)	Johnson & Wales College	6.6%
(I)	Brown University	6.0%

MAINE
    None

NEW HAMPSHIRE
(I)   Dartmouth College   4.9%

VERMONT
    None

SOURCE: Center for Statistics, U.S. Office of Educational Research and Improvement.
NOTE: For complex universities, the institutional total is reported. Thus an undergraduate college, for example, may not be reported separately from the university as a whole.
NEBHE Analysis, August 1986. (P) = public; (I) = independent.

Section Three

THE INTERNATIONAL PERSPECTIVE ON STUDENT LOANS

Sixty nations provide higher education loans for students or parents. One of the programs in Latin America began with the express purpose of making loans to Colombian students who wished to attend universities in the United States. From Sweden to Germany to Japan, most industrialized nations provide education loan assistance to their students.

The literature on education loans is very limited. The World Bank sponsored a series of reports by Maureen Woodhall of Great Britain, one of the few nations yet to adopt an education loan program but one of the best sources of information for the rest of the world. Bruce Johnstone of the State College of New York at Buffalo published an important analysis of higher education finance in five nations. His question was, "Who pays?" And what is the role of government, philanthropy, parents, and students in meeting the costs of higher education? He found that the education financing system in each nation varies widely according to the traditions of each culture.

President Johnstone spoke at the MHEAC 30th Year Conference on his findings, with special attention to the use of education loans in the several nations. What is amazing is the tremendous variation among countries. The Federal Republic of Germany, for example, charges *no interest* on education loans

87

and allows a grace period of five years after college before asking for loan repayments.

Another article on what the United States might learn from other nations grew out of an address by Joseph M. Cronin at the Harvard Graduate School of Education. He suggested that if the U.S. wants to assist borrowers in low-income occupations or public service, there are lessons to learn from Sweden, a nation with a 2 percent education loan default rate and comparatively generous education loan deferment policies.

Much of the U.S. debate on education loans is spent on details: Should the loan rates be fixed or variable? Should repayment rates be 5 percent or 8 percent? Should there be ten types of deferment or thirteen, up to $4,000 or $10,000 a year? Should bank subsidies be 3 percent or 3½ percent over Treasury Bill? Congressman Chester Atkins told a group of New England educators that he rarely found such a collection of arcane and specialized debating issues. One advantage of international comparisons is the broader perspective that policymakers can get on U.S. financial aid policy by examining the strategies of other countries.

Of course, the role of education loans depends also on the extent to which governments pay directly the cost of colleges and universities. Also, some nations subsidize the housing and food costs of university students. Only in America, Johnstone reports, do we ask parents and students to pay such high amounts of tuition for so many "independent" colleges. This discussion of higher education around the world helps us think more sensitively about the role of credit along with grants and work and other forms of government subsidy.

Chapter 7

INTERNATIONAL PERSPECTIVES: A FIVE-NATION STUDY

D. Bruce Johnstone

One of the happy outcomes of international comparative studies is the comforting realization that we are not alone, whether in our goals, our problems, or oftentimes even in our selection of solutions. But another advantage, every bit as useful, is the realization that there are often other, very different, ways of doing things. For example, nations vary in the way the costs of higher education are shared among parents, students, taxpayers, and institutions. Even though the solutions formed by one country are rarely transportable intact to another, we could do well to ponder the following questions:

- Why do British students pay almost none of the costs of their higher education, whereas their Scandinavian and North American counterparts pay, through work and loans, a very substantial share?
- Why are British, German, and French parents expected to contribute to their children's costs of living and American parents to a portion of the actual costs of instruction—at least to the extent of their ability to pay—whereas Swedish parents are not?
- Why are student loans in the United States subsidized to

the extent of about 25 cents on the dollar, compared with
about 53 cents in Sweden and about 78 cents in Germany?
Why do the students in England refuse to endorse any kind
of government-sponsored loan program, even though the
government in power clearly wants a loan program and
even though the absence of any way to borrow to cover any
of the costs of higher education causes great hardship on
those students who are excluded from the otherwise very
generous, but also narrow and selective, program of outright government grants?

My interest in the comparative study of student financial
assistance began in 1971 when I was directing the Ford
Foundation's study of the income-contingent loan concept.
That year I traveled in Europe to study student loans,
especially in Scandinavia. In 1984, while working with The
College Scholarship Service on those old questions, "Who
pays and who should pay?" I began to find some analytic
value in a paradigm of cost sharing and burden shifting.
This paradigm asserts that the costs of higher education (in
any society) are shared by four parties: taxpayers, parents,
students, and philanthropists, the latter contributing
either individually or through institutions and institutional
endowments. The paradigm further assumes the sharing to
be essentially a zero-sum game—that is, any cost or burden
that is lifted from one party must perforce be shifted to
another. From this perspective, the policies and instru-
ments we associate with student financial assistance—for
example, the calculation of expected parental contributions, the determination of "need," the setting of tuitions
(or in Europe, the great resistance to tuitions), the limits of
student "self-help," the norms and limits of student borrowing together with rates and terms for repayment—can
all be viewed as elements in a complex system that appor-
tions the costs of college among taxpayers, students, parents, and philanthropists. Changes or proposed changes in
the system may then be analyzed for their shifts of portions
of the cost burden from one party to another.

Intrigued by the possibility of applying the "cost sharing/
burden shifting" perspective to an international comparative study, I traveled to England, France, West Germany,

Sweden, and Romania, gathering information on: (1) costs of university attendance to the student and family; (2) expected parental contributions; (3) need-based grants; (4) indirect taxpayer support through subsidized rooms or meals or transportation; (5) expectation of, and opportunities for, part-time employment; and (6) student loans. In examining student loans, which are used extensively in Sweden, West Germany, and the United States, I looked for the division of the loans between the "true loan" (that is, the amount of principal that the repayment streams would actually amortize at some reasonable rate of interest or discount) and the subsidy or "effective grant" (that is, the difference between the amount borrowed and the calculated "true loan," otherwise calculated as the present value of the stream of individual repayment subsidies).

My field report, the first-ever comparative study of student financial assistance that delves into student and parental shares, was published by The College Board in 1986.[1] The judgment as to which country's system is best depends on an individual's circumstances:

- If you are a very good, full-time student, you would do well to be British. You would get free tuition and $3500 to $4000 for studying in London, with no self-help expectations.
- If you are an academically weak or a part-time or an otherwise non-traditional student, you would do well to be American. Higher education is highly accessible, tuitions are low (if not zero) in the public sector, part-time students are eligible for some grant aid, and term-time work and loans are abundant.
- If you are a parent, try to be Swedish. There is no expectation of parental support, regardless of your means or your children's choice of university. In a similar vein, if you are a married adult whose spouse aspires to higher education, you should also be a citizen of Sweden, where you will have no financial responsibility for your mate's costs of tuition or living.
- If you are going to have to borrow, try to be German. You will have five years of grace after graduation and then up to 20 years to repay at zero percent interest, with additional bonuses if you finish early or in the top 30 percent of your class.

• If you are a taxpayer, from the standpoint of minimizing your burden of higher educational expenses you had best be French. The tax-supported, per-student operating expenses of the universities are low (at least by Northern European and North American standards), the grant aid to students is minuscule, and parents must be terribly poor to qualify for any assistance anyway.

Relative Points of View

How does American higher education, especially our higher education financing, look to the Europeans? We have a set of beliefs that support a very strong and very widespread demand for higher education: the belief that education beyond high school is the entry to good jobs and social status (even if, unlike many Europeans, we have never expected a college degree to guarantee a job); the belief that higher education is a proper aspiration for most young people (one-half or more of an age group) and for very many not-so-young people; and the popular belief that the expenses of a college education constitute a good personal investment, easily justifying a financial sacrifice by parents as well as the twin burdens of part-time work and debt on the part of students. Despite these beliefs, or perhaps because of them, higher education in America is notably insulated from government and even from the power of the purse. Europeans are surprised at the absence of any true federal ministry for higher education, at the relative autonomy of even our public colleges, at the size—and even more at the influence—of our private education sector, and at the institutional competition for students, complete with marketing, salesmanship, and even price-discounting as enrollment inducements.

With regard to finance, several characteristics following from our beliefs and the structural peculiarities of our educational system stand out to Europeans: The enormous tuition costs of the private sector, the apparent willingness of parents to meet very high expenses and of students to share so substantially in the burden through part-time work and loans, the philanthropic assistance, especially in the private sector, but also increasingly in the public sector . . . and in the end the almost complete individualization of every student's total aid package to the point that the sharing of costs between taxpayer, parent, student, and philanthropist indeed specify a particular student at a particular college.

What, on the other hand, is striking to an American about European higher education, in general, and European higher educational finance in particular? European higher education is overwhelmingly public, tuition-free, dominated by a central ministry, and "politicized" in the literal sense of being buffeted by class and party ideologies and periodically shaken by changing governments. Higher education is open to a much smaller proportion of the young adult age group, although generally as a matter of "right" to all who have passed the rigorous requirements of the academic secondary track. The line between the universities, with their research orientations and high status, and the rest of higher education (the British polytechnics, French institutes of technology, and German Fachhochschulen) is sharper than in the United States, where many institutions correctly labeled "university" are nonetheless of mediocre academic status and where some that are only "colleges," or are narrowly technical, enjoy very high status.

The costs faced by students and their families in most of Europe are only the costs of student living. Estimates for the United States and the four European countries are shown in Figure 7-1. There is, of course, both within-country and among-country variation. Discounting the effect of tuition, which in Figure 7-1 impacts all of the U.S. estimates as well as the estimated cost of the French Grandes Ecoles, the costs of student living are quite similar. Costs are highest in Sweden, reflecting high costs of living there, the absence of any governmentally subsidized expenses, and a cultural view that would have a 21-year-old student live at about the same living standard as a 21-year-old clerk. Costs in Germany are also fairly high and would be higher but for the government-subsidized meals and housing. Costs to the student and family are low in France, due to subsidized meals, housing, and other expenses, as well as to a tradition of living at home and a greater acceptance of genteel academic poverty. The costs in the United Kingdom are somewhat under those of Sweden, Germany, or the United States, largely because of a considerably lower standard of living in the country as a whole, but they are a bit above those of France, because of the absence of special governmental subsidies and a tradition of living away from home if at all possible.

Financial assistance to bring these costs within reach of all able students is generally in the hands of the education ministry or of a governmentally affiliated student service organization, not of the institution to be attended. American students tend to think of their student-borne share of costs as a personal investment, for which they may well have to work part-time or borrow money, or both, but which will probably pay off. Their European counterparts tend to view higher education more as their proper calling, by virtue of their intelligence and successful academic secondary school preparation, for which the government ought to be prepared to support them much as the workplace supports their colleagues who chose not to pursue the academic track in secondary school. But there are also striking differences among the United Kingdom, French, German, and Swedish systems of sharing these costs of student living among parents, students, and taxpayers. Compare the expectations upon parents, as a function of parental income, as shown in Figure 7-2.

In the United States, the expected parental contribution begins at an annual income of about $15,000, reaches the $4000 or so contribution required of parents with a child in a public college or university at an annual income between $35,000 and $40,000, and reaches the $12,000 "plus" contribution required of parents with children in the high-cost private sector at incomes of $80,000 and up. The expected parental contribution in the United Kingdom is very similar, with slightly higher expected contributions in the low-middle-income range. Contributions level off after an annual income of about $30,000, when the expected contribution reaches what would otherwise have been the full U.K. grant of about $3650 (based on a student attending school in London in 1985–86).[2]

The expected parental contribution in France, by contrast, begins at a very low income (just over $7000) and increases at a very steep rate until the parental contribution reaches a maximum and the need-based grant is phased out entirely at an annual income still of only about $11,000. The French need-based grant is extremely small at its maximum and is given only to the desperately poor. The "ordinary poor" continue to enjoy free tuition and subsidized meals and some board, but no grants.

The Federal Republic of Germany has an expected parental contribution mid-way between the French and the Anglo-American schedules. At its maximum, it is still very low by American standards—perhaps $3000–3400 because of free tuition and subsidized room and board. But these contributions are expected at lower incomes than in either the United States or the United Kingdom, thus placing a somewhat higher burden on low- and lower-middle income families, and a lighter burden, at least as compared to the United States, at upper-income levels. The parental contribution in Germany also is not so much an "expectation" as it is a legal obligation, enforceable by the courts on the basis of action brought either by the child or the Ministry in a case of non-support.

The Swedish parent has no officially expected contribution. The dotted line in Figure 7-2 is merely a plausible assumption of what Swedish parents may contribute, either to lessen their children's debt obligations or to provide a somewhat higher living standard than is made possible by the standard loan.

Figures 7-3, 7-4, and 7-5 combine the expected parental contributions, the governmental grants (including an estimate of the subsidy inherent in the student loan), the expected or probable student contributions, and in America the probable institutional or philanthropic contributions to meet the full costs of college for low-, middle-, and high-income families. Note again:

1. For low-income families:
   (a) Relatively high amounts expected from parents in France and Germany.
   (b) Absence of a student's share for either the United Kingdom or France.
   (c) High institutional, or philanthropic, contributions in the U.S. private sector.

2. For middle-income families:
   (a) Parental share very similar in the United States and Germany, a bit smaller in the United Kingdom, and all but non-existent in Sweden.
   (b) Student share minuscule in the United Kingdom, small in France, noticeable in Germany, and large-to-huge in the United States.
   (c) Philanthropic aid in the United States important for middle-income families with students in the high-cost sector.

3. For high-income families:
   (a) Large but manageable parental share in England and Germany, small parental share in France, tiny share for the Swedish parents, and huge shares for American families with children in the private sector.
   (b) Costs in Sweden still borne heavily by students, but also by the taxpayer—in this case, via the loan subsidies available to all students.

Variations in Loan Programs

Student loans vary from an international perspective in a number of ways. First, in my five-country study, loans play an important role in three (the United States, Sweden, and the Federal Republic of Germany), an insignificant role in France, and no role whatsoever in the United Kingdom. But student loans are also used elsewhere, principally in Scandinavia (Denmark and Norway), Canada, Japan, and Latin America (especially Brazil and Colombia, but also Ecuador, Dominican Republic, Jamaica, Panama, and other countries).

Second, probably the most important difference among the loan plans is their degree of subsidy. All are, and probably must be, subsidized to some degree. I do not think that there exists an interest rate high enough to carry a truly unsubsidized student loan plan available to all students without collateral or credit checks or risk-rating. But there are different types and levels of subsidies. The principal consequence of the high degree of subsidization in Sweden and Germany is not just a shift of costs to the taxpayer; it is the resulting imperative of a strict need-based rationing—and the consequent inability of loans to serve effectively as a backstop for students denied, for whatever reason, their parental or governmental portions, or as a device to shift some consumption and living standard from the future to the present. In this light, the American GSL, especially as rates have converged in recent years, is a more flexible and useful instrument. But it is still not available, because of our need-based rationing, to the modestly affluent family who wishes the student to bear, by loans, a share similar to that borne by other students. The international perspective underscores the usefulness of a loan program that is subsidized enough to be accessible and not overly burdensome, yet also so sufficiently unsubsidized to undergird that share of costs deemed appropriate to be borne by students without the fear of its being misused and converted to cheap capital by the non-needy family.

Third, generally available student loans, at least in the United States and Scandinavian experiences, do seem to encourage or make possible a steady shift of burden from parents and taxpayers to students. At the same time, a shift of burden from taxpayers or parents to students via loans is always accompanied by a secondary shift of some burden back to the taxpayer via the governmental subsidies.

Fourth, Scandinavians have not experienced student loan default problems to the extent Americans have. Part of the difference may be in our generally greater lawlessness or in the Scandinavian's greater social and geographic cohesiveness. More important may be the very great accessibility in the United States of higher education—and thus of loans—to young adults with neither commercial credit nor academic aptitude, nor very likely a job upon graduation. I see little in the experiences of Sweden, Germany, or other European lending nations that could help us lower our defaults.

And fifth, Swedish and German loans, like the National Direct Student Loan (NDSL), are capitalized from the government's operating budget and treated like any other expenditure rather than like investment expenditures or assets. Thus, new loan capital weighs more heavily than it might on the Ministry's operating budget. Other countries, such as Denmark and Canada, rely as do we more on guarantees in the private capital market. While the latter can also distort the true costs of lending—for example, by obscuring future obligations for interest subsidies and purchases of bad debts—governmental guarantees of privately originated debt help reinforce the crucial distinctions between grants and loans.

In conclusion, it is difficult to lift intact whole or even parts of programs from other countries. Our financial aid system, including our loan programs, the state guarantee agencies, and the like, may be a monstrosity on paper. But it works reasonably well in terms of our adjustments and expectations and tolerances, and by-and-large, we can be proud of it. Nonetheless, I think we can better understand our own financial aid and loan system, like our language or our own culture, when we understand those of other countries.

Endnotes

1. Johnstone, D. Bruce. *Sharing the Costs of Higher Education: Student Financial Assistance in the United Kingdom, the Federal Republic of Germany, France, Sweden, and the United States*. New York: The College Board, 1986.

2. The United Kingdom, French, West German, and Swedish currencies have been converted to U.S. dollars, not by market exchange rates but by "purchasing power parity" ratios, which are less volatile than exchange rates and which say, in effect, that a United Kingdom grant of £ 2165, expressed as $3650, purchases in London what $3650 purchases in the United States. See Johnstone, *Sharing the Costs of Higher Education*, op. cit.

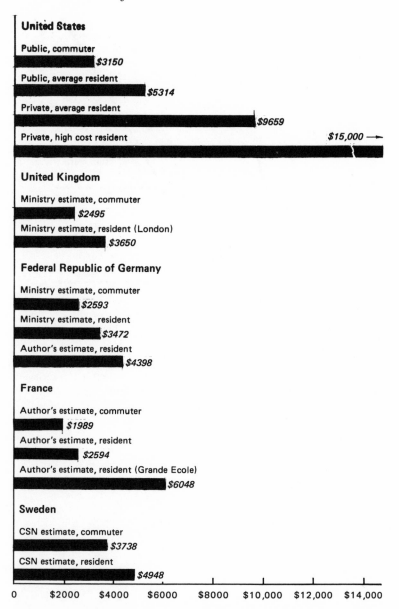

United States

Public, commuter
$3150

Public, average resident
$5314

Private, average resident
$9659

Private, high cost resident
$15,000 →

United Kingdom

Ministry estimate, commuter
$2495

Ministry estimate, resident (London)
$3650

Federal Republic of Germany

Ministry estimate, commuter
$2593

Ministry estimate, resident
$3472

Author's estimate, resident
$4398

France

Author's estimate, commuter
$1989

Author's estimate, resident
$2594

Author's estimate, resident (Grande Ecole)
$6048

Sweden

CSN estimate, commuter
$3738

CSN estimate, resident
$4948

0   $2000 $4000 $6000 $8000 $10,000 $12,000 $14,000

Exhibit 7-1   Costs Faced by Students and Their Families in the United States, The United Kingdom, Germany, France, and Sweden (various estimates, 1985-1986). *Source: D. Bruce Johnstone,* Sharing the Costs of Higher Education *(New York: The College Board, 1986), p. 146.*

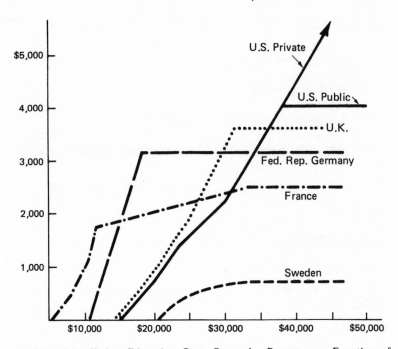

Exhibit 7-2   Higher Education Costs Borne by Parents as a Function of Family Income in the United Kingdom, Germany, France, Sweden, and the United States (1985-1986). *Source: D. Bruce Johnstone,* Sharing the Costs of Higher Education *(New York: The College Board, 1986), p. 147.*

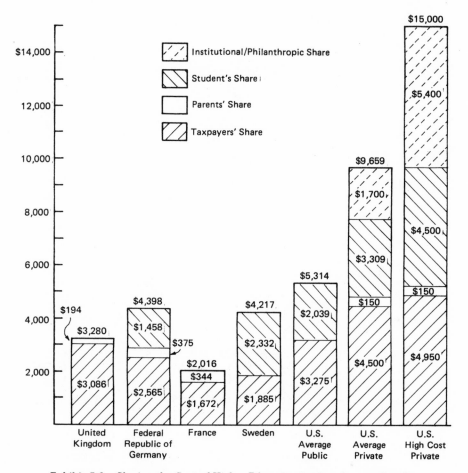

Exhibit 7-3   Sharing the Cost of Higher Education for Low-Income Families in the United Kingdom, Germany, France, Sweden, and the United States (1985-1986). *Source: D. Bruce Johnstone,* Sharing the Costs of Higher Education *(New York: The College Board, 1986), p. 148.*

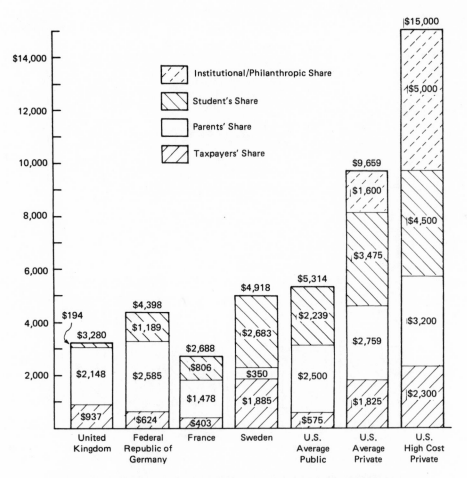

Exhibit 7-4   Sharing the Cost of College for Middle-Income Families in the United Kingdom, Germany, France, Sweden, and the United States (1985-1986). *Source: D. Bruce Johnstone,* Sharing the Costs of Higher Education *(New York: The College Board, 1986), p. 150.*

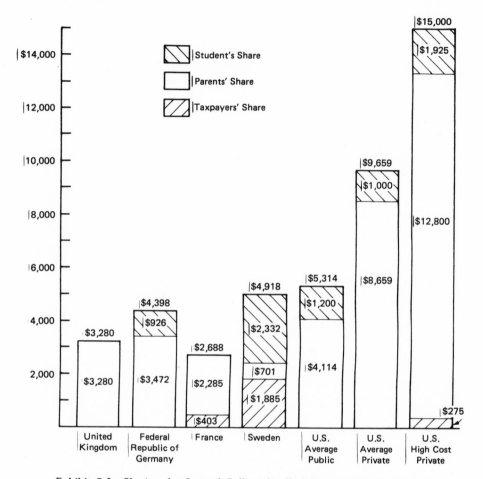

Exhibit 7-5 Sharing the Cost of College for High-Income Families in the United Kingdom, Germany, France, Sweden, and the United States (1985-1986). *Source: D. Bruce Johnstone,* Sharing the Costs of Higher Education *(New York: The College Board, 1986), p. 152.*

Chapter 8

STUDENT FINANCIAL AID: AN INTERNATIONAL PERSPECTIVE

Joseph Marr Cronin

The education loan program in America is no longer an experiment. Rather, it is an impressive commitment which measures high on the scale of assistance provided to students and higher education worldwide. In 1986 the U.S. Government passed the $50 billion mark in guaranteed student loans. Loans have become an important, even essential, ingredient of college financial aid and family financial planning. Many colleges award partial scholarships but require up to $5,000 in self-help, $2,500 in work, and $2,500 in education loans. Education at an independent college today can cost $10,000 to $18,000. Public university costs, including room and board, approach the $5,000 or $6,000 range. In short, loans are increasingly viewed as necessary, not merely convenient.

For the most part, university officials and families express appreciation for this support. Admissions officials know that upwards of a quarter of an entering freshman class could not attend without loan assistance. Families, especially those with more than one child in college, rely on loan programs to spread the cost of education over a longer time span. Loans also allow a choice of colleges, including those away from home and those with expensive specialty programs.

But, not everyone is enthusiastic. Administrators of education loan programs in the United States face the challenge of responding to the concerns of some educators about the use and abuse of loans. The College Board reports that the percentage of federal government grant and scholarship aid has declined and that the percentage of loans as a proportion of federal support has risen from 25 percent to 47 percent over the past ten years. Frank Newman, writing for the Carnegie Foundation for the Advancement of Teaching, has called for more work-study, questioning the efficiency, cost, and societal impact of loan programs. Newman finds the increasing dependency on loans alarming. He believes that the trend should be curtailed because excessive loans can inadvertently undercut traditional values. And, the U.S. Secretary of Education each year announces new and drastic measures to reduce federal subsidies for student loans. All of these misgivings follow periodic television and newspaper reports about the delinquency rate of professionals and the seizure of property owned by defaulters.

America has continued to opt for a system of higher education that is open to all. Financing the costs of such a system, which enriches both the lives of individuals and the larger society, is a fundamental policy issue. Our system of higher education finance involving a combination of work, loans, and grants has been successful. We should, however, look around the world to see how other nations address this issue.

The Experience of Other Countries

The World Bank and other international groups, such as the Organization for Economic Cooperation and Development, regularly review the experiences of many countries in financing education. Rarely used or debated in the United States, their findings are noteworthy. For example, a World Bank report by Maureen Woodhall in 1983 revealed that more than 50 nations use education loans for all or some portion of student financial aid. Japan, the most advanced industrial nation, relies on a mix of generally low tuition and student loans, not on scholarships at all. Virtually all of the Latin American nations have relied on loans to help students finance higher education. Colombia adopted education loans as national policy at the same time as the U.S. Congress adopted the Defense Education loans in 1958. One early purpose was assistance to young people who wanted to go to the United States to study.

After more than 20 years of international experience with student and family loan programs, economists and educators subscribe to a series of legitimate purposes for providing educational credit. The consensus is that loans are essential in:

1. Providing a continuing source of finance for higher education.
2. Contributing to national development by encouraging investment in education to fulfill manpower needs.
3. Promoting equality of opportunity by making it possible for poor students to finance their own education and pay for at least a portion of it later out of their enhanced earnings.

Of the European nations which make student loans, the Scandinavian countries offer the most valuable experience. One example is that, while relying on student loans, the Swedes have addressed the crucial issue of allowing college graduates to go into low-paying human service careers. The solution works this way: (1) If you enter a job paying below average wages and your income is below a minimum level, you can defer loan payments for one year at a time, and (2) students have until their 50th birthday, if necessary, to repay their loans. In fact, only 10 percent of Swedish graduates ask for a delay in payment. The loan amount is increased each year by an inflation index (for example, 4 percent) which is considered fair and reasonable in return for the deferment.

The Swedish student loan default rate is 2 percent, while the U.S. rate is approximately 10 percent. The latter may rise, the Secretary of Education worries, to as high as 13 percent by 1990. Why the difference? Consider the following:

1. The U.S. required, until 1986, most students to pay guaranteed student loans back in 10 years, except for persons in the military, the Peace Corps, and certain approved internships. Other exceptions require proof of serious hardship, total disability, or death.
2. The U.S. loads medical and dental students with up to $100,000 of education debt, most of it Health Education Assistance Loans (HEAL), then denounces their delinquency rates when at age 27, as residents, they earn only $20,000 and cannot pay $500 a month.
3. We pay teachers, social workers, the clergy, nurses, and many health workers less than is warranted by the value they add to our society. We have been underpaying tutors, mentors, and ministers since Puritan times. Japan pays teachers at salary levels comparable to those of accountants and engineers.
4. We allow a six-month grace period to establish oneself financially, while the Swedes allow two years and the Federal Republic of Germany allows five years.

Solutions to the Problem

Despite concern about the $2 trillion debt or the $150 billion annual deficit, reasonable adjustments in those areas should be debated in the Congress. Education loan payment solutions could include the following three measures: (1) Extending debt repayment periods for longer than 10 years for those with heavy indebtedness or those who opt for human service professions, a recommendation the Congress accepted in 1986; (2) allowing graduated repayment, with a lower payback amount in the early years and higher repayment amounts in the later years; and (3) supporting higher salaries in all the helping professions for both women and men—that is, the economic structure must change, specifically the salary scales for state and local workers such as teachers, nurses, and social workers.

The Carnegie Foundation's Newman report suggests that loan programs be curtailed and work programs expanded, implying that working one's way through college is an American ethic. Newman's central point, that more American youth must prepare for public and community service, is excellent and uncontestable, but it would be unwise to pit loan programs against work programs.

During the first half of this century, a person could indeed work his or her way through college. Five hundred dollars a year paid for all education costs. Doing so today is not impossible, but it is extremely difficult to study full time and work more than 10 or 15 hours a week. Hundreds of thousands of young and older students are doing this right now. Incredibly, The College Board discovered that some urban university students do work 30 to 40 hours a week and carry three or four courses a semester. However, they have little time for the library, cultural events, public service internships, new friendships, or campus life. No one recommends that much work or such diminution of the broader learning experience.

One model that does work well is the Cooperative Education Program pioneered at Northeastern University in Boston. Nine thousand five-hundred students, a majority of the undergraduates, study for a quarter, then work for 13 weeks. They learn and earn, alternating study and work. Do they need loans? Yes, Northeastern students borrow, since they need funds for books, clothing, personal expenses, and transportation to a workplace, as well as tuition of $6,000 to $7,000 a year. In fact, Northeastern students borrow more GSL dollars than students in any other private college in Massachusetts.

Should loans be forgiven for work? The World Bank reports, for instance, that student loans in Honduras can be written off in part for service in priority areas such as rural development. Twenty-seven U.S. states have passed student loan forgiveness provisions to recruit teachers. Will this work? After Sputnik, the United States tried loan forgiveness incentives to recruit more teachers. Unfortunately, this experiment (1958 to 1968) resulted in relatively few teachers staying in the classroom more than five years and, except for teachers of the handicapped, the federal loan forgiveness feature was dropped. A College Board study (1968) concluded that it was fundamentally unsound to create a situation in which a student might choose a career on the basis of loan forgiveness. Actually, 91 percent of the 142,000 teachers with education loan indebtedness said they had planned to go into teaching anyway. By 1990 the states with loan forgiveness programs will know whether they are enough to attract and retain teachers or whether teachers' salaries must be raised. Perhaps both measures are necessary. Loan forgiveness schemes must not be used in any way to perpetuate the low salary levels which neither attract nor retain enough good teachers. Indebtedness has not discouraged dedicated teachers as much as reductions in workforce and other retrenchment measures.

The Congress, and many educators, worry about "an appropriate balance" between self-help and government help, grants, work, and loans. The popularity of loans, and the proportion of loans to grants, has risen substantially since 1977. Why? First, Congress and the voters like self-help programs as a supplement to scholarship grants. The loan programs provide "self-help" for working class and middle-income families. The ethic holds that loans are not "give-away" programs like grants. The participation of three million students a year in this area represents substantial growth, one-quarter of all students in postsecondary education. Second, the notion of loans is attractive as an economic investment. Loan programs for the government are approximately one-third to one-half as expensive as grant and scholarship programs. Federal appropriations of $4 billion leverage $9 billion in new loans, with the capital coming from banks—a leverage rate of 3 to 1. Of course, when interest rates are high, a subsidized loan becomes as costly as a grant.

Strategies for the Future

Important questions about work, support systems, and responsibility remain. How can the United States convert knowledge of the international experience into strategies for fine-tuning our student loan system? And, what are the prospects for Congress finding an appropriate balance among loans, grants, and work? There is, of course, no perfect balance. Low-income students receive more scholarships and government-supported work, while middle-income students often have access to only loans and private work-study jobs. Thousands of college students will continue to rely on a combination of the following sources:

1. *Parental contributions:* remain a very important source of help for one out of two students today.
2. *Work:* already expected of hundreds of thousands of college students (both summer work and term-time work). A federal work-study program is available for low-income students, and an increasing number of states offer work programs in both the public and private sectors.
3. *State scholarship programs:* New York, Pennsylvania, Illinois, and the New England states among others, have increased this help.
4. *Employer-supported scholarship programs and employee education:* Half of all college students now are over 21, and many receive help from their employers.

Loans are a necessity for many students—currently, at least 3 million a year. Of great importance to the public policy debate is the information that few students borrow more than $7,500. Many, in fact, borrow for only one or two years of education. The average indebtedness is less than $5,000; the average default is $3,500. Doctors who borrow amounts in five or six figures are very much the exception.

Can students repay their loans? Nationwide, 90 percent of them do. The more education, the lower the default rate; the more one borrows, the better the percentage rate of collection. Should two debtors marry? There is no reason for them not to, when one considers their combined incomes. Concerns about "negative dowries" fade when both partners work for two or three years. Maureen Woodhall notes that British critics of loan programs continue to voice concern about their negative impact on women, but that nations with student loan programs have not found them to be a problem in this regard. There are

two exceptions which the Congress addressed in 1986: the
need for new parents to have a deferment, and help for
parents with a severely disabled child. Can borrowers
enter the career of their choice? Student loan indebtedness
is not responsible for the current Yuppie enthusiasm for
well-paying jobs. In 1978 only one in four students had
taken out a loan; as of 1985 that proportion has not risen.
But what is excessive debt? The lifetime earnings of today's
average college graduate will be one million dollars. (Of
doctors, two to three million dollars.) When there are
genuine problems of debt burden, as in public service jobs,
three solutions can be enacted into law:

1. A longer repayment term than ten years. The Swedish
   approach to grace periods and occupational deferments
   makes sense. Health loans in the United States can be
   repaid over 25 years, which provided a useful precedent
   for education loans.
2. Graduated repayment of loans, with lower payments during the first three to five years and higher payments
   toward the end.
3. Partial or full forgiveness of loans for public service or
   scarce supply professions. The military currently offers
   some of the best programs of loan forgiveness and educational severance benefits.

The World Bank study by Woodhall offers an important
insight on the true cost of loan programs. Many nations
marvel at finding that a new subsidized loan program costs
only $10 to $15 for each $100 lent. Of course, the second
year there must be a subsidy for another year of loans and
in the third year there will be defaults. In the beginning, a
government cannot economize on staff to monitor the
program, or else funds or borrowers, or both, will disap-
pear. Even without subsidy, an education loan program
will eventually cost more than 30 cents for every dollar
lent. With a high degree of subsidy and loan forgiveness
features, the cost of loan programs can escalate to 60 cents
of every dollar lent.

The World Bank discovered that most countries begin a
loan program with the government itself making the loans.

After some years, government officials report difficulties getting the money back and banks are called in to take over the tasks of loan origination and collection. More experienced than government agencies at this specialty, banks can keep costs and default rates low—if they are involved from the beginning of the cycle.

What else can we learn from other nations, from OECD and the World Bank reports? First, loans are more efficient than grants. Frank Newman has expressed concern about the long-run costs of loans, but research for the National Commission on Student Financial Assistance found otherwise; after inflation, the borrower in repayment paid very little for his or her loan. And the nation obtains twice as much aid for every dollar spent on loans than for a dollar spent on any other form of government assistance. Second, we can see that loans are not a panacea. Low tuition, grants, and scholarships remain a very strong source of education assistance in dozens of nations. And finally, reliance on work is an almost uniquely American approach. Most nations consider university study itself work. Loans reduce the need for half-time or full-time employment at low salaries, and they can be repaid later when the borrowers earn more. The concept of investing in one's education because it will engender greater earning power later is crucial.

Of course, it is important to recognize the limitations of loan programs. First, certain trades and occupations do not pay enough or place enough of their students to avoid a high default rate. Lower-level clerks, beauticians, and household workers cannot afford much debt. U.S. policy on loans should take this fact into account. Second, students should not borrow all the money required. Parents or spouses can help share the borrowing burden and provide a better repayment stream. The federal PLUS loan program will gradually become a strong source of assistance. Third, loans may not be compatible with multiple degrees or with long, drawn-out, part-time study. The World Bank contends that, in fact, loans foster efficiency: Students do not stay at the university taking graduate courses as long as once was the fashion. Similarly, an eight-year course of part-time study may not allow heavy reliance on annual borrowing.

Some critics complain that the current U.S. education loan program is very complex. There are 12,000 lenders, 58 loan guarantee agencies, and many specialty firms and contractors. But complexity is not an evil. There are, after all, 15,000 school districts, not 50, and access to 14,000 neighborhood banks remains a valuable service. The federal loan program is complex in part because the United States likes decentralized banking, because consumers need protection, and because taxpayers need ways to avert fraud and abuse. Also, Congress felt that a guaranteed loan program with state agencies could render faster service to students and lenders than a centralized program such as the Federal Insured Student Loan of the 1970s. Of course, many administrative features could and will be streamlined in the years ahead.

The current loan program is costly. But a $3 billion program that provides $8 or $9 billion a year in new loans is cost-effective. Costs must and can be trimmed. There is debate about whether so many students should have access to subsidized loans, or whether subsidized loans should be restricted to those with documented need. And, there are questions about loans being used not only for degree-granting colleges but for short-term technical schools whose students need low tuition and/or direct grants.

Loans will never be as popular as outright grants, but attending college on credit is respectable. What must be avoided is an unproductive debate over work versus loans, a centralized national program versus an effective state-based program, and excessive rhetoric over defaults which can be reduced, if not totally eliminated. Instead, we can learn from the international experience—from nations which can teach us how to build better cameras, safer motor cars, and a more efficient system of allowing college graduates their choice of career.

Section Four

SUPPLEMENTARY SOURCES OF SUPPORT

The key to the availability of education loans is the willingness of most of the 14,000 lenders in the United States to provide loan funds. Education lenders include commercial lenders, savings and loan associations, cooperative and savings banks, credit unions, and several dozen colleges who lend a portion of their endowments, often under the guarantee of federal and state loan agencies. During the 1960s lenders were virtually on their own in making loans—no government reinsurance until 1967, no secondary markets until 1973, and very little support except from a handful of small private loan guarantee corporations, mostly in the eastern states.

The original notion of a small loan, perhaps $500 to students to be repaid within five years, no longer provides enough assistance or enough time for repayment. Today, a lender making a million dollars in new education loans a year can find a portfolio of five, ten, twenty million or more building up. In response to the problem of finding money for new student loans, Congress in 1973 created the Student Loan Marketing Association (Sallie Mae) to purchase loans and advance funds to lenders for new loans. Between 1975 and 1985 two dozen states established their own student loan secondary markets for similar purposes. Lenders found the availability of secondary markets extremely useful to obtain the liquidity needed.

Another option tested in the 1980s was that of asking parents to assume additional responsibilities for aiding students. One vehicle is the parent loan for education, authorized by the Congress in 1980 and available since 1981. One problem with the parent loan is the limit of $4000 per parent per student. Especially in the Northeast this sum is too little. A supplementary or family loan was created to meet the need for loans up to $10,000 or $15,000 for undergraduate education costs, with parents making payments. A new guarantee agency, The Education Resources Institute (TERI), provides the framework for this program.

The other new frontier for younger parents is called tuition futures, a choice of educational savings or investment plans. As of 1987 each state is studying how to develop these options, essentially a format for education financial planning. But some critics of Campus Futures indicate a preference for a regional or national approach to preserve choices for each family and each child.

These organizational and financial innovations suggest a more complicated world of educational assistance than ever contemplated in the 1950s. But the stakes are much higher in the 1980s—not $600 a year, but $16,000 per year, with up to $40,000 a year by the twenty-first century. The following chapters suggest some future trends which include greater use of parent or family education loans.

Chapter 9

THE PROSPECT FOR FAMILY EDUCATION LOANS

Ernest T. Freeman and Thomas D. Parker

Most of us have encountered a member of an older generation who is at once in awe of and skeptical of higher
education. Self-made entrepreneurs, for example, have
long worried that higher education would "spoil" the next
generation. At the same time, most of these older skeptics
have insisted that the next generation receive the highest
possible degree of education. The current generation of
"Yuppies" would be surprised to know that, as recently as
the 1950s, many corporate executives or small business
owners had no advanced degree and indeed often no
college education. The college graduate as the norm in
America did not emerge until the GI Bill of Rights made
college possible for large numbers of those previously
unlikely to attain higher education. Prior to World War II,
only one in every 17 young adults graduated from college.
However, not having a degree or being suspicious of
elitism in no way dampened the insistence of parents that
children and grandchildren receive degrees.

In the 1980s there is a similar paradoxical attitude on the
part of an older generation of corporate executives, most of
whom have received one postsecondary degree (usually an
AB in the liberal arts), toward the bright young men and
women working for them, most of whom have received

both an undergraduate degree and a graduate degree in business or engineering. The stories repeat in different ways, but the pattern is always the same. The older generation with less education suspects that the newer generation may not be as savvy or as aware of the importance of "sweat equity" as it should be, but at the same time there is the understanding that, sooner or later, increased educational attainment is an economic as well as social necessity.

What is less widely understood is that this pattern of constantly increasing educational attainment from generation to generation has been made possible only by a *combination* of support for education by federal, state, private, and parental sources. Some parents prefer not to acknowledge the degree to which outside support enabled their offspring to attend college, but outside support has come not only in the form of aid to individuals in cases such as the GI Bill of Rights and the Guaranteed Student Loan Program but also in the form of aid to educational institutions—for example, the land grant university system and state support for colleges and universities. Philanthropic contributions long subsidized prices at private institutions, and such support kept the price of education low at many institutions. For a period spanning two decades, from the 1950s to the mid-1970s, this combination of support for education enabled many students to obtain higher education with minimal family assistance. The fact that many students were able to "work their way through" college on the basis of meager summer and term-time earnings is not so much a tribute to personal diligence as it is a reminder of how the price of education was kept low by the combination of support systems mentioned above.

What is emerging in the 1980s is a pattern of uncertain federal and state support and steady increases in the price of education. The result is that the historical pattern of substantial family assistance is re-emerging. In the mid-1960s it was hoped, with the creation of the Guaranteed Student Loan Program, that reliance on family assistance would be unnecessary if the student would take on a minimal loan burden. The fallacy of this assumption was documented clearly in the early 1980s by the Sloan Commission Report on Higher Education authored by Carl Kaysen and Kenneth Deitch. They argued that students alone could not be expected to continue to take on the loan burden to offset increasing prices and that a return to family assistance would be necessary. The College Board estimates that 65 percent of all students receive parental assistance.

In the next decade, the fundamental policy issues facing higher education finance will revolve around achieving a new balance among sources of support for students and educational institutions. The argument here is that one of the resources clearly emerging in this balance is the non-federal alternative loan. A combination of political and economic forces are at work which will result in either diminished federal funding for higher education or at least very slow growth in such aid. This reduction coincides with a period when prices in higher education continue to rise. What follows is an attempt to describe and analyze these forces and the way in which they impinge upon alternative loan trends, including a description of the actual workings of one such alternative loan program devised to meet the new needs. The Education Resources Institute (TERI) serves as a case study exemplifying problems and prospects in the field.

The Political, Economic, and Policy Background

In its 1986 reauthorization of the Higher Education Act, Congress steadfastly resisted those who would have severely diminished the federal Guaranteed Student Loan Program. Yet, veteran observers of the interaction between political forces and federal support for access to higher education remain concerned about fluctuations in public opinion and in the views of political and policy leaders in Washington, D.C.

Washington policy analysts have long been critical of certain aspects of the Guaranteed Student Loan Program. More than a decade ago, Chester E. Finn, Jr., now Assistant Secretary of Education for Research and Improvement, in his book *Dollars, Scholars, and Bureaucrats*, laid out the basic case for eliminating the GSL within state-based guarantee agencies and substituting a national student loan bank with complete student loan administration emanating from a Washington, D.C. bureaucracy. Arthur Hauptman, a respected consultant in financial assistance policy, has advocated replacing the GSL with a modified version of the National Defense Student Loan program. Michael McPherson, Professor of Economics at Williams College and a former Brookings Institution fellow, critiqued the use of private capital markets in the federally assisted GSL program. These and other technical analysts emphasized economic and bureaucratic inefficiencies in the program. The complexity of the GSL, they argue, has become so great that tinkering with its provisions to make them more efficient is not enough. They support dismantling the GSL as presently constructed and replacing it with a new program.

Just as policy analysts both left and right are raising serious reservations about GSL, politicians along the entire ideological spectrum are raising concerns. There is a widespread perception that students are borrowing too much, that private enterprises are profiting too greatly, that default rates are too high, and that the availability of federally subsidized loans discourages higher education institutions from attempts at cost containment. While all of these criticisms are either untrue, unproven by any research, or greatly exaggerated, the fact that many believe them cannot be ignored.

These opinion trends indicate that the need for alternative non-federal sources of education loans will continue in the coming decade. The so-called "alternative" or "supplemental" loan program initiatives (meaning alternative or supplemental to federal GSL funds) are not new. The Congress itself recognized the need for supplemental loans when it established the "PLUS" program authorizing additional loan funds for parents and students beginning January 1, 1981. By January 1982, the number of alternative loan programs in existence was large enough to warrant the establishment of a newsletter reporting on them. "The Alpine" published its first issue under the auspices of the Alternative Loan Program Task Force of the National Council on Higher Education Loan Programs and the Massachusetts Higher Education Assistance Corporation. The conventional wisdom in 1982 was that the demand for education loans to supplement GSL and PLUS would be filled largely through state programs using tax-exempt revenue bonds for funding. This notion was reinforced by the fact that in 1982 in Massachusetts, PLUS loan volume declined by 36 percent, due largely to Congressional action raising the interest rate from 9 percent to 14 percent.

A dozen states created tax-exempt revenue bond programs to provide education loans at lower interest rates, and many believed that they would replace the PLUS program entirely. But this was not to be. The Congress progressively tightened restrictions on the issuance of state-based, tax-exempt revenue bonds. The interest rate on PLUS loans dropped from 14 to 12 percent. Within a year, Massachusetts PLUS loan volume grew by 25 percent. In the 1986 reauthorization, the Congress revised the sluggish formula by which the PLUS rate had previously been established and replaced it with a more sensitive variable rate formula to assure that PLUS could be more competitive with the general market. The effect of the new PLUS program is yet to be measured; however, most analysts believe that PLUS volume will increase. The Congress also in 1986 established Supplementary Loans for Students in an attempt to improve on the PLUS program for independent students which had at one point unfortunately been dubbed "ALAS" (Auxiliary Loans to Assist Students).

The overall message from the 1986 reauthorization of the Higher Education Act is that the U.S. Congress does not support the draconian measures for reduction in federal student aid assistance proposed by some analysts and by the Reagan Administration. Astute lawmakers on both sides of the aisle have realized that this battle over support for student assistance is not merely a matter of how much to cut the budget. The fundamental policy issue is the degree to which the U.S. Congress and the electorate to which it reports believe that widespread access to higher education is a major national priority.

The Education Department during the Reagan Administration has formulated a series of responses to the issue. Initially, the Department embraced the PLUS program as a healthy alternative to GSL. Its rate of interest was higher, so costs to the government for special allowance payments to banks were substantially lower than GSL. In addition, it had no post-deferment "grace period" to subsidize. It was seen by officials in the Department as a potential replacement for guaranteed student loans to middle- and upper-middle-income students and parents.

While none of the drafters of the original PLUS legislation imagined that PLUS would be the cornerstone of a future Republican Administration student financial aid policy, it became that in 1981. The democrats in 1979–1980 saw PLUS as a supplemental source; they never envisioned that it would be used substantially to replace GSL assistance. The 1978 Middle Income Student Assistance Act, which provided for guaranteed student loans to all regardless of income, was based on the premise that all students have a right to postsecondary education. The PLUS program as envisioned by the Reagan Administration in 1981 assumed that education was a privilege to be provided for students by parents if they were willing to take on the concomitant responsibilities.

In the years since 1981, legislators from both parties have abandoned the "loans for all" concept of the Middle Income Student Assistance Act. Eligibility for the Guaranteed Student Loan Program has been severely restricted. The effect of the 1986 reauthorization and its new eligibility requirements are such that on many campuses financial aid officers are predicting reduction in guaranteed student loan volume by 25 percent or more. The market rate PLUS or SLS programs become the only federal loan alternative for vast numbers of middle-income students previously served by GSL. For these students, the fact that loan limits for upper classmen in the GSL program have been substantially increased is of little solace.

PLUS may be an adequate replacement at low-cost institutions for students displaced from GSL. The fact that the price of higher education has risen since 1980 at a rate more rapid than inflation, however, means that fewer and fewer institutions can boast such a low cost that PLUS will be able totally to replace GSL. In addition, an unsubsidized PLUS loan, with interest deferred, will cost a student more than a GSL.

This analysis demonstrates another reason why the need for non-federal alternative loans will increase dramatically. In the past, the non-federal alternative loan programs have served largely upper-middle-income students and parents at high-cost institutions. The removal of GSL eligibility from the middle-income layer, along with the increased prices at most institutions, mean that alternative loans will increasingly become a necessity if widespread access to higher education is to continue.

These shifts in the demographics of borrowers will have an effect at the institutional level as well. For postsecondary institutions with substantial portions of operating income coming from the Guaranteed Student Loan Program, the issue is less one of social policy regarding access and more one of institutional survival. At the campus level, the implications of a reduction in student loan availability are substantial. Private and public institutions both will feel the impact. Private colleges have higher prices and rely more heavily on loans to enable families to pay tuition bills. Public colleges and universities with lower prices argue that the formulation of eligibility requirements penalizes institutions with low prices because the high cost of education is one factor driving the amount of loan eligibility.

Another significant result of diminished eligibility for GSL is that many postsecondary institutions discover that some students, especially in the private sector, cannot come up with money to pay for full-time study. Obviously, the number of such students increases as eligibility for subsidized federal loans decreases. Institutions, therefore, are eager to guarantee the availability of alternative loan funds for students and families.

Many institutions initially believe that they can provide alternative loans by establishing their own programs or joint programs with a local lending institution. The student loan business, however, is considerably more complicated than it might first appear to a board of trustees or a financial aid office. In the NDSL loan program, colleges and universities were asked to administer and service student loan portfolios; the results were all too often negative. Institutions which have for many years had effective small-scale loan programs using institutional funds have, as the demand for alternative loans has increased dramatically, been forced to turn to outside sources for help in loan administration and collections.

In Massachusetts, for example, such requests for assistance from colleges began arriving at the Massachusetts Higher Education Assistance Corporation in the early 1980s. By 1982 the corporation saw fit to establish a planning team made up of lenders, university representatives, and the corporate strategic planning department to design a prototypical non-federal alternative loan program. MILO, the Middle Income Loan Option, was the first design for such a program by a state guarantee agency. Between 1982 and 1986 many new alternative loan programs were developed. Few prospered. The market for these programs was not great in the face of GSL and PLUS availability.

The combination of the new restrictions of 1986 and increased college prices created an alternative loan program market. Yet, just as the alternative loan market accelerated, policymakers and educators voiced concern that students and their parents were having to borrow too much to pay for the price of higher education. Economists studying the value of human capital offer reassurance about the lifetime value of education purchased vs. debt burden assumed. Americans, however, are accustomed to only minimal borrowing for education. There has emerged a tension between the natural interest of the private sector to increase education loan product volume and concerns by leading educators that this zeal should be tempered with debt counseling and caution about borrowing.

The TERI Response

In Massachusetts, the borrowing dilemma has been addressed by establishment of a private, non-profit institution, The Education Resources Institute (TERI), which is governed jointly by representatives of the lending community and the educational community. TERI's mandate is to provide an alternative loan program *and* information, counseling, and research. The purpose of TERI is to address social and educational issues related to the need for new sources of capital funding. Its charter states: "The Corporation shall always be operated exclusively for charitable and educational purposes through assisting students in attaining an education and through assisting educational institutions in providing an education in an economical fashion." This rather broad mandate enables the corporation to adapt to changes in the student financial assistance universe. The breadth of the mandate, however, did not keep the drafters of the charter from also making rather narrow technical provisions to encourage the Institute in the establishment of an attractive alternative loan program. Section (b) of Article 2 of the corporate charter is noteworthy in that it offers a glimpse into the complexities of the alternative loan business. This section allows TERI:

> . . . to make contracts, give guaranties, and incur liabilities, including any secondary liability by way of guaranty or endorsement of the obligations of any student, his parent, or guardian, or of any educational institution; borrow money at such rates of interest as the corporation may determine; issue notes, bonds, and other obligations; and secure any of its obligations by mortgage, pledge, or encumbrance of, or security interest in, all or any of its property, or any interest therein, wherever situated, for any of the purposes of the Corporation.

The above dramatically illustrates the need for a specialized institution capable of dealing with the complicated interface between students, educational institutions, lending institutions, and institutions of public finance.

After one year of operation it is possible to summarize how TERI has been able, using its complex charter language, to establish a program for the benefit of students

and educational institutions. In essence, in its first year
The Education Resources Institute established the TERI
Supplemental Loan Program. This program enables cre-
ditworthy families to borrow up to $15,000 annually to pay
education costs. Despite the considerable analysis indica-
ting that there was need to provide families with increased
ability to borrow for education, the waters in the fall of
1985 were largely untested. After nearly two decades in
which family borrowing had been only minimally necessary outside of the federal programs, neither TERI analysts
nor marketing experts at major banks were certain about
the future of alternative family education borrowing. A
number of lending institutions were approached with the
TERI idea. The institution willing to accept the risks
attendant to being a pioneer was the Bank of Boston, which
made a significant commitment of personnel and capital. It
contributed a substantial marketing effort on behalf of the
TERI guaranteed program which at the Bank of Boston was
designated "The Alliance Loan Program." The first Bank of
Boston Alliance loan was disbursed in November 1985. In
return for its willingness to be the pioneer and take the
risks of entering the market first, the bank realized volume
of ten million dollars in the first year of the Alliance
program.

The Institute has subsequently entered into detailed
agreements with a total of seven Massachusetts lenders
willing to offer these loans to students at favorable interest
rates in return for the TERI guarantee that, in the event of
default, lenders will be reimbursed. This marriage of a
private, non-profit institution and banks willing to make
private capital available for students is a model which many
consider to be a prototype for higher education finance in
the 1990s and beyond. Unlike other models being developed and tested, the TERI program does not require
educational institutions to participate in the inherent risks;
nor does it charge a fee to educational institutions. Families declared ineligible for federal guaranteed student loans
by tighter eligibility restrictions have welcomed the availability of the TERI loan as a replacement. Others, espe-

cially in the graduate and professional schools, have been able to supplement federal loans with a TERI loan to enable them to meet high graduate school costs.

Further, the TERI charter with its combination of a broad mandate and specific technical, financial language has ensured TERI flexibility in the creation of loan programs. Even in its first year, the Institute developed, in addition to its basic program, two other models for supplementary financing. Together with Boston College, TERI shaped the EXCEL program to provide family loans up to $15,000 a year, demonstrating that the basic TERI model could be adapted to the specific needs of a single institution. In addition, TERI joined with Nellie Mae, Inc. and the Consortium on Financing Higher Education (COFHE) to demonstrate that a group of colleges and universities with similar interests and needs could band together to ensure that their supplementary loan requirements were met in the best possible way. This TERI, Nellie Mae, COFHE program is entitled SHARE. The SHARE program serves a consortium of thirty schools nationwide including New England institutions such as Amherst College, Brown University, Dartmouth College, Harvard University, the Massachusetts Institute of Technology, Mount Holyoke College, Radcliffe College, Smith College, Wellesley College, Wesleyan University, Williams College, and Yale University.

The combination of features in the TERI loan program has proved attractive. These features include loans of up to $15,000 annually; independence from federal funding, including no needs test requirements and no income limits; independence from federal bureaucratic paperwork, making the TERI loan vastly more convenient and less expensive to administer for schools and banks; long repayment terms of up to 15 years; and options to pay interest only while in school. Analysts believe that this combination of features accounts for the fact that, in its first full calendar year of operation, the program made available more than $20 million to students throughout the United States—a figure considerably in excess of original estimates. The willingness of families to participate even more in the financing of their children's education was confirmed during TERI's first year of operation.

The popularity of the TERI loan program in its first year was due at least in part to the fact that the TERI concept attempts to address the full range of social and individual problems emerging in the transition from a period when society required relatively little participation in higher education finance by parents to a time when parents must participate more. The TERI concept is that providing additional loan assistance solves only a portion of the emerging set of problems. To address issues other than supplemental loan availability, the Institute has undertaken an ambitious program of activities designed to inform and guide students and their parents to ensure that access to higher education remains feasible for future generations.

The Higher Education Information Center at the Boston Public Library is a division of TERI. Since January 1986 the Higher Education Information Center has helped more than 10,000 individuals gain access to higher education through its on-site counseling and information services, a toll-free hotline for information on higher education, careers, and financial aid opportunities, and workshop services held in community and school locations. The Higher Education Information Center provides a model for public/private partnership, helping young people and adults gain better access to higher education. The Center encourages participation in higher education by providing people with free information and advice on schools, financial aid, and careers. Services are directed particularly to people who are unfamiliar with the financial aid and college admission processes.

The Center is recognized as a national model in providing information and counseling, because it has been able to coordinate the efforts of and attract support from a wide variety of institutions. It is funded in part by contributions from 25 Boston area colleges and universities which value its ability to provide urban students with information about educational opportunity. The Massachusetts state legislature, through the Massachusetts Board of Regents for

Higher Education, has recognized the value of the Center with a grant of $190,000 to expand its toll-free information hotline and to develop special programs in six urban communities to inform high school students about higher education opportunities. The Boston Public Schools have recognized the Center by offering a grant to enable the Center to provide special programs for Boston students including college bus tours, early awareness programs, and a career/school exposition.

At the federal level the U.S. Department of Education, through the Fund for Improvement for Post-Secondary Education (FIPSE), has financed the development of a peer advisor program to train Boston Public School graduates to conduct workshops for ninth and tenth graders on educational decision making and planning. In addition, federally sponsored educational opportunity centers rely on the Center for services to students. Other contributions to the Center have come from businesses such as Digital Equipment Corporation, which recognizes the importance of the Center's activity, and from non-profit associations such as the Massachusetts Association of Student Financial Aid Administrators (MASFAA). The Boston Public Library and the Roxbury Community Action Program in Boston both have made contributions in kind toward the Center's activities. The Center asked M. L. Carr of the World Champion Boston Celtics to assist the Center through volunteer public service announcements.

One of the Center's outstanding achievements involved participation in the development of the Action Center for Educational Services and Scholarships (ACCESS). ACCESS has gained national recognition by providing Boston public high school students with financial aid information and college advice as well as with "last dollar" scholarships for students who receive insufficient aid from other sources to cover school costs. Both ACCESS and the Higher Education Information Center received crucial initial assistance from the Massachusetts Higher Education Assistance Corporation.

These "non-loan program" features make TERI unique and have attracted considerable attention to the TERI model. Other initiatives planned by TERI for assistance beyond providing loans include:

1. Early awareness programs about financial aid and the promotion of planning in financing education, including pamphlets, posters, cablevision, and other audio and visual techniques.
2. Loan counseling and default reduction programs for participants in education loan programs.
3. Training of financial aid administrators, including contracts or grants to professional organizations.
4. Assistance to persons who have education loans but who, because of below-average salary or public service commitment, face severe difficulty in making loan payments. These programs include options for interest rate buy-downs, graduated repayment programs, and the restructuring of loans on a private basis.
5. Enhancement of education loan origination and processing technologies for lenders and educational institutions.

The TERI model of combining financial services and counseling and training will not be easily emulated by for-profit financial institutions. Similarly, state and other not-for-profit institutions established for purposes of making loan monies available to students through tax-exempt sources will have a difficult time matching the features of the TERI loan program. State tax-exempt authorities are increasingly unable to compete with other state needs for tax-exempt money under federally imposed limits for each state. State and tax-exempt sources have also traditionally imposed fees and other liabilities on educational institutions in return for participation in education loan activities. The TERI loan program assesses no fees or other expenses to educational institutions.

Given the fact that a wholesale revision of federal and state systems of support for higher education is unlikely in the near future, that state tax-exempt programs have the limitations outlined above, and that private for-profit lending institutions are generally unable to address the issues of training and education about debt burden and debt management, the TERI model is attractive. Economists, public policy analysts, and experts on massive federal assistance programs will all continue to produce detailed and valuable studies outlining what could be, given different political and historical forces or given the sudden availability of massive amounts of federal funds. In the meantime, the TERI model of how a private, not-for-profit institution can cooperate with private, for-profit lending organizations to produce both capital availability and guidance and information for individuals is in place and working well.

Chapter 10

IMPROVING STUDENT AID

Joseph Marr Cronin and Sylvia Quarles Simmons

Although education loan programs by and large work well in America, problems remain. This chapter addresses the issue of how to convey higher education information to low-income children and adults, one of the most challenging problems in any culture. For example, how can higher education recruiters convince a student living in a public housing project that a better life is a probable result of attendance at a community college, a technical school, or a university? Educators, bankers, and business people in Boston have tried to grapple with this question and to invent new ways of reaching out to those unaware that college is affordable. Most of these efforts have taken place since 1981, the highwater mark of federal assistance to education. The inventions of the Greater Boston Chamber of Commerce, creation of the Boston Compact, the higher education work group, and the Boston Plan for Excellence in the Public Schools (including the ACCESS program) are described in detail.

The chapter concludes with some recommendations to policymakers on how to integrate education loan policy with scholarships and with public service and career planning in a more thoughtful and constructive fashion. Education loan programs are complex and, like any vehicle, require fine-tuning and adjustment to travel any distance.

133

Extending Opportunities for Higher Education in Boston

One of the best strategies for helping students attend college is supporting them through the complex process of applying for admission and financial aid, including loans. The maze of required paperwork unreasonably challenges most parents the first time they face the Financial Aid Form (FAF) with its specific questions about family assets, costs, and special needs.

Parents of college-bound children in the middle-class suburbs usually manage to fill out the forms or search out the answers about eligibility for financial aid. Many parents in the city, however, give up: they do not even try, or do not know where to get help. This is one reason why the suburbs send as many as 80 percent of their high school graduates on to college, while city school systems send less than half of theirs. Indeed, given their high dropout rates, cities send as few as one-quarter of those who attended school through the sixth grade, resulting in a great loss of talent.

There are solutions designed to respond to this problem. The major federal program of assistance is called TRIO, an array of Upward Bound, Talent Search, and Educational Opportunity Centers (EOC) located in many states. Many colleges sponsor Upward Bound programs enabling high school students to visit colleges, then spend a summer on a campus to taste college life, and to get considerable adult and peer group support in preparing for college. Talent Search represents an effort to locate gifted and talented students, many of whom do not realize that some colleges are looking for applicants exactly like themselves. The Vermont talent search program sends a college counselor to each high school in the state and actively recruits students for college, informing them about educational opportunities and available financial aid.

The EOC is a federally sponsored program designed to provide advice on higher education and financial aid mainly to adults 19 years of age and older. Low-income people receive advice and assistance in finding a college or technical program and the grants and aid to pay for it.

Massachusetts offers all of these programs plus the campus "special services" of tutoring, remedial classes, and counseling support. Even so, the number of inner-city students actually making their way to college is, in Boston and other cities, far fewer than some educators thought possible. What should be done?

In 1981 Robert R. Spillane became Superintendent of Schools in Boston. Just before his arrival *Time* had characterized the Boston schools as a "national disgrace." The school system decline could be traced to the 1930s when enrollment peaked at 135,000, then dropped by 50,000 prior to the enactment of the racial imbalance law, and decreased another 30,000 during the 1974–1982 years—a pattern similar to the decline of many urban school systems with or without desegregation plans. Spillane sought help for his city school system from business corporations, unions, and universities. Massachusetts Higher Education Assistance Corporation (MHEAC) responded by recruiting and training citizen volunteers who helped high school counselors inform students about financial aid information. Jody Cale, Assistant to the President of MHEAC, recruited these citizen advisers from School Volunteers for Boston. The Massachusetts Association of Student Financial Aid Administrators (MASFAA) also participated. MASFAA was already recognized through its sponsorship of a speakers bureau and financial aid month (usually January) with a toll-free hotline for students or parents with questions.

During 1982 the Boston Private Industry Council (PIC) announced a new initiative to bring the public schools and the corporate community together. The PIC proposed an economic compact in which business firms would hire Boston youth in the summertime and provide jobs for high school graduates on the condition that school officials do the following: (1) raise attendance rates to about 90 percent (from the mid-80s, which was deemed unsatisfactory), (2) increase the percentage of high school graduates, currently 55 percent, by five percent a year, and (3) raise the achievement test scores of all students. The Boston Compact required Boston schools to provide a small staff and selected Robert Schwartz, on loan from the University of Massachusetts, as director. Fourteen "work groups" were formed, one of them the Higher Education Work Group chaired by Jody Cale of MHEAC and assisted by School Volunteers staff, The College Board (New England regional office), and university representatives including admissions and financial aid officers.

Meanwhile, the Greater Boston Chamber of Commerce formed an education committee comprised of the Boston Superintendent, the Chancellor of University of Massachusetts–Boston, the President of Roxbury Community College, a dozen educators, and a diverse group of business leaders. Dr. Robert Sperber, Assistant to the President of Boston University, and Harry Johnson, community relations officer for Polaroid, proposed a subcommittee to pursue corporate scholarship gifts. Because Boston University had already announced a policy of giving four-year full scholarships for each of the 17 city senior high schools, and because the Chamber Education Committee Chairman was President of the Massachusetts Higher Education Assistance Corporation, this idea quickly won acceptance. Another advocate was the Chairman of the Chamber of Commerce, Kenneth Rossano of the Bank of Boston, who previously had established a private scholarship program for vocational education students called STRIVE. The Chamber also raised funds each year for the Program for Academic Youth in School (PAYS).

Both the Compact work group and the Chamber subcommittee searched for effective strategies and outside resources. The workgroup sought and obtained a $70,000 Cox family trust grant to plan and establish a Higher Education Information Center where potential students could obtain admissions and financial aid advice. One issue in establishing a center was to find in a neutral site (neither a public nor an independent college) where the information would be provided. City Hall was one option. Would a public library be too staid? The New York City Library, for example, had offered a special reference area with books on college aid, on colleges and universities, and on careers—

all within twenty-five steps of one another at the Fifth Avenue–42nd Street annex.

Another issue was coordination and staffing. The Chamber subcommittee invited Clarence Mixon of the Cleveland Scholarship Federation to Boston to explain his experience with a very successful annual fund-raising campaign that offered financial aid counselors free to the Cleveland public schools and at a modest fee to parochial and suburban schools. There, counselors promoted student use of all the state and federal aid programs. If all the grants, work, and loan options fell short, "last-dollar" scholarships could be provided to meet remaining need. Companies and foundations provided the money not only for the last-dollar grants but for the counselors and a small administrative and fund-raising staff. The Chamber group felt this model could be adapted for Boston.

During 1984 and 1985 the two initiatives grew together. MHEAC served as the fiscal agent; the Boston Public Library was chosen as the Higher Education Information Center and ACCESS site. Mayor Ray Flynn, the Library Board, and Senate President William Bulger all provided support. Dr. Ann Coles from North Shore Community College was recruited to direct the Center, raise funds, and develop a staff. Initial sources of the funds were:

1. A Cox family trust start-up grant of $70,000.
2. Funds ($50,000 a year) from MHEAC for providing loan information.
3. A voluntary assessment of $80,000 from twenty colleges and universities represented on a Presidents' Steering Committee.
4. The transfer of the site of a Boston Educational Opportunity Center from the YWCA to the Boston Public Library, a federal project worth $100,000 a year.
5. Funds from the Bay State Skills Corporation for a Career and Learning Line, literally a financial aid CALL service.

The year 1984 was also the 200th anniversary of the Bank of Boston. After consultation with university and philanthropic experts, the Bank chose to establish an urban education fund called the Boston Plan for Excellence in the Public Schools. A gift of $1.5 million made possible school improvement grants of $100,000 a year to Boston Public Schools whose faculty and principals wrote school improvement grant proposals. Soon afterwards other companies made contributions to middle school athletics and academics (John Hancock Mutual Life Insurance Company) and to teacher fellowships (The Bank of New England).

In May of 1985 Chairman Rossano unveiled a plan at the 75th Annual Meeting of the Greater Boston Chamber of Commerce. With education the theme, it was a very upbeat gathering of 1,000 persons. Ken Rossano and Chamber President James Sullivan announced the new counseling and last-dollar program as the Action Center for Educational Services and Scholarships—ACCESS for short. The New England endowed the ACCESS program with $1 million, enough to generate funds to help as many as one hundred Boston high school students obtain advice and the last one hundred or five hundred dollars needed to attend college. These "last dollars" were added to a base that built on Pell grants, state scholarships, guaranteed student loans (31 percent), and work-study programs.

Edward E. Phillips, Chief Executive Officer of The New England, made his gift part of the Boston Plan for Excellence and was appointed chair of the ACCESS Subcommittee. Later he agreed to raise additional funds and persuaded The Boston Foundation to offer a $1 million challenge grant. During 1986 corporations pledged another $2.5 million to the ACCESS program.

Meanwhile, the General Accounting Office filed a report with Congress on state education loan agency reserves, suggesting that some of the older agencies, such as in Massachusetts, had accumulated excess reserves. The MHEAC Board proceeded to lower the bank reserve requirement and student fees and to give $3 million to other groups, $1 million each to (1) ACCESS (earmarked for loan counseling for Boston school students through The Boston Foundation), (2) The Higher Education Information Center, and (3) ACCESS/HEIC programs elsewhere in the state of Massachusetts. The MHEAC gifts were in the form of endowments, the interest earnings on which could be used to pay for loan information and counseling services. MHEAC was guided by two important convictions: First, that persons from low-income families often need a great deal of help—even convincing—in applying to colleges and in completing the documents for financial aid to meet the costs of education. And, second, that if the federal government were to limit the use of previously unrestricted reserve funds, then the board and staff intended to provide information assistance to persons who needed help to attend higher education programs.

By 1987 endowment funds of $5.5 million for ACCESS and $2 million for the Higher Education Information Center were built up. In the summer of 1986 Ted Phillips announced that the endowment would be able to provide (1) counseling and last-dollar support for public high school students, and (2) a commitment from Boston employers that ACCESS scholars would, upon graduation, be given priority consideration for hiring for professional and managerial jobs in Boston companies. This bold mixture of opportunities for urban youth electrified the nation, gaining media coverage by the *Wall Street Journal* and the *New York Times* as well as by the "Today Show," Cable News Network, and all three major network evening news shows. For many months, other city mayors and Chamber of Commerce officers deluged Boston with requests for details on how to set up similar programs.

Initially, skeptics raised questions about the commitment of Boston businesses. In the 1970s Boston had drawn negative reviews for public resistance to court-ordered desegregation of the schools and for other racial incidents. At that time twenty business corporations agreed to join in partnership with Boston high schools in support of school improvement efforts. The Boston Compact was still another effort in 1982 to marshall corporate support for a better educated workforce. The Boston Plan for Excellence and ACCESS represented a new effort to endow "in perpetuity" school improvement and access to higher education for two reasons: First, to improve the quality of life in Boston and also the reputation of Boston as a progressive, positive place in which to live; and, second, to improve the quality of the workforce of the city.

Will high school financial aid counseling and information be enough? The ACCESS counselors work with individual students and parents in filling out the financial aid information forms. However, many students need basic assistance in preparing for SAT and ACT tests or in visiting area colleges, including those in suburban settings that they might not have seen in the course of their lives in the city. With the help of a federal Postsecondary Education (FIPSE) grant (1984–1987), HEIC provided trips to colleges.

HEIC director Ann Coles agreed with The College Board assessment that grades 11 and 12 are too late to be informing students about college opportunities. She launched an "Early Awareness" program to help students in the upper elementary and middle-school grades. The children of suburban college-educated parents know that algebra is the crucial math decision by grade eight, whereas a city child whose single parent struggles to pay the basic bills may consider algebra a useless subject if the price of college attendance exceeds the family income. Early advice on courses thus can lead to an early commitment that can help make college attendance possible. The College Board Commission on Pre-College Guidance and Counseling (*Keeping the Options Open*, CEEB, 1986) concluded that, unless students are made aware of the advantages of higher education in grades 7–10, they may avoid the academically challenging courses required for college.

The Higher Education Information Center was mentioned positively in the final College Board Committee report, which recommended:

- Providing a program of guidance and counseling during the early and middle years of schooling, especially for students who traditionally have not been well-served by the schools.
- Strengthening the collaboration among schools, community agencies, colleges, businesses, and other community resources to enhance services available to students.
- Establishing a process in each state to determine the guid-

ance and counseling needs of specific student populations
and giving support to local initiatives that address these
trends (pp. 5–6).

The State of Massachusetts agreed with these recommendations and in 1986 appropriated $100,000 to support the
Higher Education Information Center and another
$90,000 to support awareness and information projects
with similar purposes around the state. Also, the City of
Boston contracted with HEIC to provide up-to-date training to the 41 guidance counselors in the Boston schools
who need to keep up with the rapidly changing state,
federal, and private loan and scholarship programs. The
College Board concluded that schools have "too few counselors trying to do too much for too many," (p. 12) and
noted that the clinical (professional) training for most counselors is no longer adequate for these expanded responsibilities.

For Massachusetts the EOC, HEIC, and ACCESS programs represent a series of steps aimed at expanding the
number of low-income youth and adults entering higher
education. Other solutions—health, employment counseling, day care, pregnancy and family counseling, nutrition,
drug rehabilitation—play just as fundamental a role. Educators and corporations must continue their partnership in
developing links from grade school to high school to college.

Sharing the Responsibilities for Debt Management

Chapter 1 challenges the allegation that U.S. students are
borrowing excessively, cannot pay back their loans, and are
destined to involuntary servitude to the banks and their
collectors. Dennis Martin and Joseph Boyd's study (discussed in Chapter 2) shows that U.S. students can pay back
their loans without undue stress if they have a salary of
$16,000 or more, which is at or below entry level wages in
most occupations requiring an associate or bachelor's degree. But what of exceptions: The young lawyer with
$30,000 in debt who wants to take a low-paying job as a

public defender or legal advisor to poor people; the doctor with a debt of $80,000 incurred after attendance at a highly selective and expensive liberal arts college followed by an even more expensive private medical school; the relatively inarticulate high school dropout who tried again to pursue education at a secretarial or cosmetology school but did not complete the program?

We contend that the U.S. Congress, the states, colleges, and lenders have set up a program that serves the 90 percent of students who need to borrow reasonably well. In the late 1980s, amounts will range from $10,000 to $25,000. There are cases, of course, at either end of the income and indebtedness spectrum that require special handling and sensitive adjustment to government and banking policy. Congress recognizes total disability as a legitimate reason for loan default and temporary disability as a reason for deferment. Tales of hardship faced by women raising infant children alone persuaded Congress to defer payments for young parents. At present, the U.S. Congress recognizes many different special circumstances with provision for deferment, exemption and postponement of payment, as follows:

1. Service in the Peace Corp, Vista, or ACTION.
2. Service in the U.S. Military (although most officers are quite able to make as much of a payment as beginning school teachers or social workers).
3. Service in the National Oceanographic and Atmospheric Administration Corps (NOAA).
4. Service in U.S. public health agencies.
5. Enrollment in part-time or full-time course of study.
6. Enrollment in an approved graduate fellowship program.
7. Enrollment in a rehabilitation training program.
8. Service as a full-time teacher in a public or private elementary or secondary school in an established teacher shortage area.
9. Service in an internship required to receive professional recognition in order to begin professional practice.
10. Caring for disabled spouse or dependent.
11. Seeking but unable to find full-time employment.

12. Parental leave caring for newborn or newly adopted child.
13. Mothers of preschool-age children just entering or re-entering the workforce and earning not more than one dollar above minimum wage.

There are, of course, limits to our national compassion. People have little sympathy for doctors and lawyers who, it assumes, will qualify for $35,000 and, eventually, $100,000 annual salaries. And there have been some abuses. When attorneys in the late 1970s advertised openly in news media that they could show borrowers how to declare personal bankruptcy and thereby discharge their obligation to pay a student loan, Chapter 11 closed that loophole, amending it to make student loans non-dischargeable. Another example is provided by certain individuals diagnosed as totally disabled by psychoneurosis, who, after their loans have been forgiven, regain their health, find a good job, and earn as much as $50,000 a year.

At the same time, a number of young professionals who want to serve a low-income clientele are discouraged by the requirements of the education debt repayment system. Universities can sometimes make concessions in the name of serving community interests, such as providing special scholarships to those who commit all or an early portion of their career to public service and providing subsidy for or suspension of loan payments for those who enter public service. Harvard Law School in 1987 announced the expansion of a program which forgave loan payments for graduates who accepted a public service job at less than $20,000 a year and partial subsidy or reduced payments for those who accepted similar jobs at less than $29,000. The Kennedy School of Government at Harvard created a similar program. Not all universities can do this. Some large law firms allow a portion of their young associates' time to be spent on "pro bono," or public service assignments, including the service of indigent clients or associations of poor people with few funds to pay for legal services. More law firms could set up a pool of funds either to help young lawyers pay back loans or to free more of them for public service assignments.

Many medical doctors gravitate to metropolitan areas where the quality of life and level of compensation is high, even though the medical profession has made efforts to improve the distribution of doctors to rural areas and to smaller cities having an inadequate supply of doctors. It must be considered, though, that thousands of these junior practitioners are entering the profession with $100,000 loan indebtedness and $500 to $1,000 a month payback schedules. The Southern Illinois University Medical School in Springfield, Illinois worked to link underserved communities to young doctors who were admitted to a "family practitioner" program, the latter-day equivalent to the general country doctor. Communities involved in the program often provided access to housing, membership in clubs, and other amenities to convince medical recruits that they would be appreciated in their service to those in need of medicine.

Two dozen states have authorized loan forgiveness programs for those who wish to enter public school teaching. In 1986 the policy office of The College Board reviewed these policy solutions designed to encourage talented men and women to enter the teaching profession. One typical format is the forgiveness of $2,000 or $2,500 of loan for every year devoted to classroom teaching, up to five years. The College Board study reported some surprising perspectives. First, an earlier study of the experience of teacher loan forgiveness in the 1960s found that almost 95 percent of the teachers would have entered teaching anyway and simply borrowed higher sums when they learned of the forgiveness option (Irene Spero, The College Board, D.C., 1986). And, second, in many states the number of loans forgiven is quite low. Another concern is whether the existence of loan forgiveness programs perpetuates low salaries, since wage scales are a fundamental deterrent to teacher recruitment. Also, a five-year loan forgiveness program will not promote retention of math and science majors who have more lucrative options in other careers. If we want to attract superior people to teaching, New York State Education Commissioner Gordon Ambach argues, then we should offer substantial fellowship programs—at the $10,000 level for masters degree candidates.

Additional Opportunities for Program Changes

The Guaranteed Student Loan Program has many strengths, has been enormously productive, and has the potential of becoming even more useful in the future. The future of the program and the future of financial assistance can be strengthened through support of the following ten recommended improvements.

1. *Increase Grant and Scholarship Programs.* State and Federal governments should offer a strong program of basic grants and scholarships as the bedrock of educational opportunity. Loans should not become the major source of student financial aid for low-income and working-class youth. To this end:

(a) Low-income (below $10,000 family income) students should be made eligible for Pell grants of up to $6,000 by 1990.
(b) State scholarships of up to $5,000 should be available to these students.
(c) Supplemental student grants should be available to able students admitted by very selective schools.
(d) Graduate school scholarships of $10,000 should be made available for national priorities such as public health, social services, and the training of teachers in mathematics, science, and other subject ?reas in which there is a teacher shortage.

2. *Offer Special Grants to Meet National Shortages.* The federal government should offer special scholarship grants to 10,000 future medical doctors, dentists, and veterinary doctors each year who pledge that they will spend twenty years of their lives in family practice in preventive medicine, or in rural or low-income urban areas with a practitioner shortage documented by a state health agency or manpower agency.

Medicine amply rewards most surgeons, the specialists, and those who affiliate with the great teaching hospitals and university medical schools. We are a well-to-do country, we pay most doctors well, and they can and do pay their loans back. But many doctors are needed on Indian reservations and in remote rural areas, barrios, and ghettos. Those dentists and veterinarians who take low-salaried

public service jobs should qualify for $15,000 annual grants
to avoid excessive debt.

3. *Establish Grants for Part-time Students.* Adult
part-time students should be allowed to complete a bachelors degree without heavy reliance on education loans.
New York City educators have urged Congressman Mario
Biaggi to lead a crusade to make all Title IV Higher
Education Act programs open to part-time college students, including loans. Mandating access to a loan component for all part-time students, however, is probably a
mistake. Many are employed and their tuition often is, or
should be, paid by the company or agency which employs
them. Those who are unemployed or on welfare or who are
the working poor should be eligible for scholarships,
grants, or tuition waivers. Loans are not an economic,
efficient, or sensible way to pay for the part-time education
of a person who may require many years to complete a
degree. If the government would have to subsidize the
interest on a loan for eight or more years, it might be more
cost-effective to make it a grant. Loans make better sense
as a device to enable or to encourage full-time study and a
reduction of work at low wages in order to qualify for a
higher paid position in the more immediate future.

4. *Expand the TRIO Program.* The Talent Search/Ed-
ucation Information Services and special services programs
sponsored by the U.S. Department of education should be
expanded. This "trio" of programs, which includes the very
successful Upward Bound program, state or specialized
talent search counseling programs, a network of Higher
Education Opportunity Centers, and provision of extra
tutoring and counseling services for low-income youth and
adults, must be expanded. Indeed, only a fraction of
eligible youth from the bottom third of the family income
spectrum feel that they can afford college. Extra encouragement, information including bus or van trips to colleges, and early awareness programs are needed—for example, those that have been endorsed by the College
Entrance Examination Board and developed by the Vermont Student Assistance Commission, the Higher Education Information Center in Boston, and many other agen-

cies. The TRIO appropriation should be tripled, not halved as the Office of Management and Budget each year from 1982–1987 has recommended.

5. *Offer Both Subsidized and Unsubsidized Loans.* The federal government should provide guarantees for two types of student loans: (1) subsidized loans for undergraduate students attending degree-granting schools and one-year certificate programs with good-to-excellent placement records and public service graduate programs; (2) unsubsidized loans for parents, spouses, and graduate students in law, business, medicine, and engineering, because most of them will qualify for good-to-excellent jobs with above-average incomes. As recommended previously, certain medical, dental, and veterinary medical students and other helping professions should have substantial grant funds so that they can choose lower-salaried public service positions.

6. *Share Responsibility for Loan Counseling.* Colleges for many years conducted "exit interviews" for those students about to leave or graduate who have a campus loan— usually a National Direct Student Loan—to pay back. Generally this consists of a group counseling session with an explanation of students' borrowing rights and responsibilities, including an admonition to graduates to budget one's income and expenditures prudently with loan payment obligations kept in mind. Banks in many communities used to provide a comparable service for Guaranteed Student Loan borrowers, often upon entrance to college and at the time of the signing of a promissory note. With the increased popularity of banking by mail—even by computer—this face-to-face loan counseling encounter is less feasible. Lenders told the Congress in 1986 that they typically do not see the borrower at all; indeed the student applicant might be hundreds or thousands of miles away. Despite these changes and the complexity of service delivery, the need for counseling continues:

  (a) Elementary and secondary schools should explain to young students the American banking system, the nature of credit, the sanctions and penalties on loan delinquencies and defaults, and the value of a good credit rating when applying for loans for a dwelling and other consumer products later.

(b) Colleges and universities should stress the differences between grants and loans, should provide at least a group counseling session on entrance into college as well as exit from college, and offer follow-up assistance to students in obtaining employment—including re-employment—after a layoff or economic recession.

(c) State loan guarantee agencies and servicers should provide free pamphlets, counseling materials including video cassettes and personal budget worksheets, and detailed information on loan deferments, hardship forbearance, loan consolidations, and other options.

(d) Government officials and media should stress the positive statistics of the 90 percent who repay and not dwell exclusively on delinquency and default statistics to defame the program.

7. *Promote Family Education Loans.* The federal government should promote family education loans. Parent loan limits should be expanded so that the federal government can reinsure education loans of $10,000 or more per student attending the higher cost colleges and universities. In 1986 Congress increased the parent (PLUS) loan limits from $3,000 to $4,000 a year, the only increase since 1980 when the program was authorized until 1991 when, ordinarily, the next reauthorization is scheduled. This modest 25 percent increase over a ten-year period was totally inadequate to parents of students at independent colleges and universities with costs of education at $12,000 a year or more.

During 1988 Congress, with support from several concerned national associations, expects to review the loan limit for family education or parent loans. This $10,000 parent loan recommendation may actually be too conservative. Family education loans in a dozen states provided by the New Hampshire Higher Education Assistance Foundation, by Nellie Mae, by The Education Resources Institute, Inc. and by others already offer $15,000 or more per year per student with as long as 15 years to repay.

8. *Identify State and Local Sanctions for Defaulters.* When the U.S. Congress decided to direct the Internal

Revenue Service to offset or divert the income tax rebates of student loan defaulters, this action sent an important message to those who thought the federal government would play a passive or even forgiving role. As of 1987, as many as 14 states authorize a comparable tax offset action on state income tax rebates. State laws to recover education loans can also include these measures:

(a) Speeding up the process of garnishing a percentage of employee wages—for example, up to 10 percent of the monthly income of defaulters.
(b) Providing for the timely exchange of information from state revenue agencies including place of business, current home address, and phone number of those borrowers who have "skipped" out on a loan, moved, and hope they are lost for all time. State motor vehicle and revenue agencies keep excellent current information on millions of citizens.
(c) Holding up or having the power to cancel the licenses or practitioner certificates of those who must obtain a document from a state licensing board, conduct trade, or practice a profession.

Local or metropolitan agencies can also provide timely information and support regarding their employees or the whereabouts of other persons who defaulted on their education loans.

The stakes are high. If $50 billion has been provided to students in the form of loans and up to 10 percent of the borrowers have defaulted on those loans, the nation and the colleges have lost $5 billion in taxpayers' money and other forms of financial aid. The student loan default rate can be cut by half—possibly by two-thirds or more—by aggressive federal and state action and cooperation from other agencies as outlined above.

9. *Redefine Postsecondary Education Institutions.* As Bruce Johnstone has noted in his research on financial aid systems in other industrialized nations, the United States is almost unique in defining postsecondary education so broadly. In Europe, higher education and state grant and loan programs extend only to universities and very technical institutes such as engineering schools. In the United

States, the definition of postsecondary education and eligibility for federal loans expands to include secretarial schools, barber schools, beauty academies, and schools for paper hangers, tractor-trailer drivers, and dog groomers. These schools have generally been criticized for their default rate, but some have excellent placement and loan payback records. Many enroll a much higher percentage of veterans, minorities, and handicapped and low-income persons. Eligibility for Pell grants and guaranteed student loans often runs to 60 percent or even higher at some schools.

The number of specialized schools and students attending proprietary schools has risen dramatically. In the state of Pennsylvania between 1974 and 1984, the numbers rose from 4,400 to 30,000, an increase of almost 600 percent. Concomitantly, default rates for proprietary school borrowers can run to 10, 20, even 50 percent. The Illinois State Scholarship Commission regularly publishes default rates by school each year. The default numbers by school deserve more thoughtful debate.

Policy options for government action ought to include the following:

(a) Separation of the postsecondary certificate programs from the degree programs, so that loan limits can vary and default statistics be compared and contrasted by categories of schools and programs. Simply stated, degree program loan default rates ought not to be mixed with those of certificate and short-term programs.

(b) Measures to make ineligible those schools with unacceptably high defaults. Schools with low placement rates and default rates of 20 percent or higher should be declared ineligible after certification by a state loan agency.

(c) A sequence by which grant funds are assigned to students initially, with a loan authorized only after a month or two of attendance. Many borrowers default after the first few days or weeks, creating severe recovery and rebate problems for school, lenders, and agencies.

10. *Support Further Inquiry and Research.* In 1980 Congress decided there were too many unanswered questions about student aid and created a National Commission

on Student Financial Aid to collect and analyze data. For example, many citizens worried that students with high debt faced the greatest likelihood of default. Congress was somewhat relieved to find that the more debt, the more education, and the more likely a student is to make payments.

Few issues in higher education are as vulnerable to hearsay, speculation, and uninformed opinion as is student borrowing. Janet Hansen reviewed research for the Joint Economic Committee of the Congress in 1986 on the question, "Student Loans: Are They Overburdening a Generation?" She found much public concern about "mortgaged futures" but very little analysis and hard information. The U.S. Department of Education will conduct a multi-million dollar survey of student borrowers in 1987–1988 which may help fill the data gap. The NASFAA study reported on by Dennis Martin will be replicated in other states to answer some of the questions about the impact of borrowing. But many other questions about education loans remain unanswered, such as:

(a) What types of income-contingent or income-sensitive loans will work and with what types of students? Secretary Bennett's proposal of authorizing $10,000 in loans per year to students was sharply criticized. But should not the multi-year experiment authorized by the Congress move forward to see how and whether an income-related payment program can work? Should the nation look at the Yale University loan program created more than a decade ago?

(b) Are forgivable loans for teachers or other public servants a good idea? A report by Irene Spero of The College Board suggests that there may be problems in using loan programs to attract talented newcomers to teaching and that few state officials have reviewed the careful evaluation of earlier teacher loan forgiveness programs during 1958–1968. Not only the efficacy of forgiveness of loans but the utility of grants versus loans in attracting, training, and holding talented teachers should be looked at very carefully.

(c) What else can be offered to needy graduates beside forms of work, grants, and loans? Many students must borrow

just to meet the cost of room and board, which can exceed
$4,000 a year for undergraduates in a college dormitory
and twice that amount for married graduate students.
Bruce Johnstone's study, *Sharing the Costs of Higher
Education*, mentions that other nations offer highly subsidized meals to college and university students. Although
the United States does not know what to do with its
agricultural surpluses, it has, during the 1980s, systemati-
cally cut back school food programs and has virtually
outlawed the use of food stamps for college students.
What is reprehensible in America is reasonable and edify-
ing in the nations of Europe which Johnstone studied.
Research such as his on other nations can lend important
insight into forms of financial aid or subsidy and the ways
in which other nations help students and families cope
with college costs.

(d) What types of savings and investment plans would be
most useful and popular with parents preparing for the
year 2000 and beyond? Will the growth of "futures"
programs reduce the need for financial aid or reduce the
support for those too poor to save for their children? Can,
as Governor Blanchard of Michigan suggests, companies
give college future tuition money for entire sixth grade
classes in a community to motivate their completion of
school and consideration of college? How else can we
reduce the high dropout rate of children in cities—often
as high as 50 percent—and counsel them to higher education opportunities? Will programs such as ACCESS for
Boston Public School students expand opportunities,
awareness, and attendance? Will we need, as Charles
Desmond of University of Massachusetts–Boston argues,
urban scholar programs that provide cost-of-staying-in-
school stipends to adolescents with talent but no discretionary income, no allowance, and many basic financial
needs unmet at home?

Numerous other student aid issues have been insuffi-
ciently studied, such as the effect of loans on student
retention in college (opinions and findings differ), on marriage (the negative dowry issue), on subsequent career
choice (although students who do not borrow seem to be
choosing the same rewarding careers). Debate about the
issues is very healthy, but it should be informed by data

and policy analysis, especially because we are investing in our youth, our citizenry, our culture.

In writing this book we could have chosen to include information from the grim reports on "mortgaging a generation" or views which propose that "dependence on loans is alarming." Instead, we decided to make available the research on what actually happens and works—the reality of education loans. Expecting that the quest for wisdom and balance in perfecting our education system is ongoing, we included criticisms and comments on unmet needs so that policymakers may address them in subsequent deliberations. Legislators deserve our appreciation, as do the thousands of financial aid officers, lenders, directors, and reporters who have contributed so much to the development of educational loan and information programs. With them, we have been challenged in helping the first million students in Massachusetts obtain three billion dollars in loan assistance. The next generation of student and parent borrowers will present a comparable challenge.

Appendix

MHEAC DOCUMENTS

Information about ACCESS, HEIC, and the MHEAC Loan Counseling Task Force

Continuing Commitment
to Education

This booklet tells the story of ACCESS, a financial counseling and tuition assistance program to help graduates of the Boston public schools overcome the financial difficulties that prevent all too many of them from going on to post-secondary schools.

ACCESS is the result of the Boston business and academic communities working together toward a common goal. By addressing areas of broad concern, the program has quickly gained the support of many area businesses and foundations.

We in the Greater Boston business community believe that ACCESS is an undertaking of the highest purpose and feel privileged to be associated with it as corporate sponsors.

Its funding signifies our commitment to an agreement—a compact—between the public schools and the business community to improve the opportunities of students.

Our goal is to assure that any academically qualified student not be denied a higher education because of financial circumstances. Our hope is to build a better future for all.

Edward E. Phillips

Edward E. Phillips
Chairman and Chief Executive Officer
The New England
Chairman, ACCESS

NOTE: This section is a reproduction of a 1986 ACCESS publication.

The Need

Many graduates of Boston's public high schools find access to higher education difficult.

As they approach graduation, they know they need training beyond the high school level to qualify for a good job, but they can't find all the money to go on to post-secondary school.

Tuitions have risen about 50 percent in the last four years. It now costs $7,575 a year at Northeastern; $10,950 at Boston University; $11,800 at Massachusetts Institute of Technology.

Tuition trends
Undergraduate studies *

School	82-83	83-84	84-85	85-86	86-87
Harvard	$8,195	$9,035	$9,800	$10,590	$11,390
MIT	8,700	9,600	10,300	11,800	11,800
Univ. Mass.	1,128	1,128	1,208	1,296	1,296
Northeastern •	5,100	5,745	6,300	7,575	7,575
Boston Univ.	7,175	8,300	8,996	10,100	10,950
Boston Coll.	6,000	6,800	7,475	8,200	9,120

* Figures represent tuition only
• Freshman tuition only

Federal assistance is declining. For example, the Pell Grant Program, largest of the six major federal financial aid programs from 1974 to 1981, has decreased 18 percent for Massachusetts students. Substantial decreases are also expected in the Guaranteed Student Loan Program.

Many institutions can no longer provide substantial assistance. Costs are rising faster than income from endowments. Some post-secondary schools have had to dip into operating funds to keep their scholarship programs afloat.

Nobody stands to lose more in this financial crisis than the students of the Boston Public Schools.

Like students in all of America's largest cities, Boston Public School students are among the least able to pay. According to U.S. Census figures, more than 43 percent live below the poverty line. For Blacks and Hispanic students, the figures are even higher.

For nearly all Boston Public School students, post-secondary education without financial assistance is simply out of the question. The situation is so discouraging that many students who have the ability to do college work don't even finish high school.

School Department figures show that less than a quarter of the students entering the ninth grade eventually go on to post-secondary education.

Financial comparisons

A comparison of income and poverty levels of families with children under 18 years old by race or ethnic group for Boston and Massachusetts.

Income levels

The median income of families in Boston with children under 18 years old is significantly lower than the median income of such families statewide in Massachusetts.

Race or ethnic group	Boston	Massachusetts	Percentage difference
White	$17,550	$21,883	20
Black	10,541	11,918	12
Hispanic	7,793	9,166	15
Asian	20,809	21,307	2
American Indian	7,474	12,838	42

Poverty levels

The percentage of families in Boston with children under 18 years old with poverty-level income is significantly greater than the percentage of such families with poverty-level income statewide in Massachusetts.

Race or ethnic group	Percentage Boston	Percentage Massachusetts
White	8	5
Black	36	21
Hispanic	89	33
Asian	37	7
American Indian	41	20

The need for information

What most of these students and their parents don't know is that financial help for post-secondary education is very often available—if they knew where and how to apply for it.

Thousands of scholarship, loan and grant programs are offered by the federal and state governments, universities, and social, civic, religious and business organizations.

The trouble is that students often don't know how to find these sources or how to apply for aid. Financial aid application procedures are complicated. Students can't complete the applications without help.

A recent study, conducted under the auspices of the Boston Compact, found that "the multiplicity and complexity of financial aid application forms contribute to student and parental confusion and resentment toward the financial aid system."

In short, many able students miss the opportunity to go on to post-secondary education simply because they don't know how to find sources of aid and how to make out the applications.

The only real personal assistance now available to Boston Public School students is through their guidance counselors. However, there is only one counselor for every 367 students, which means that the average time for individual guidance is less than an hour a year.

Lack of money and financial information continue to plague many students, even if they do manage to get into a post-secondary school. A recent study shows that less than four percent of Boston Public Schools graduates receiving financial aid dropped out of post-secondary school before completing the first semester. Twenty-seven percent of students receiving no aid dropped out during the same period, and only 51.2 percent registered for the spring semester.

The study concluded: "Students without any form of aid have significantly lower chances of staying in college...Neither individual performance nor demographics is the critical factor influencing college retention. What matters is money."

Area colleges respond

Recognizing the financial crisis facing Boston students and their families, 25 area colleges and universities offered to help the city find solutions.

In November 1983, they signed an agreement with the Boston Public Schools, under the aegis of the Boston Compact, to improve the opportunities for graduates to enroll in higher education.

Soon a broad-based committee, operating under the aegis of the Greater Boston Chamber of Commerce, was at work formulating plans for a program to provide financial assistance and information to students.

Financial assistance to launch the operating part of the program came from the Massachusetts Higher Education Assistance Corp., Polaroid, the Boston Foundation, and the Greater Boston Chamber of Commerce.

The committee included representatives of the Boston Public Schools, the Boston Compact's Higher Education Work Group, the Massachusetts Higher Education Assistance Corporation, Hope Talent Search, Freedom House, School Volunteers for Boston, the College Board, the Steering Committee of the Boston Area College and University Presidents, and the Massachusetts Association of Student Financial Aid Advisors.

The result of the committee's deliberations was a proposal to establish a program called ACCESS (Action Center for Educational Services and Scholarships), patterned after the highly successful Cleveland (Ohio) Scholarship Program.

The program has three goals:

• Encourage students who may not have considered post-secondary education to seek out advice on opportunities;

• Assist public high school seniors in applying for financial aid;

• Provide "last-dollar" scholarship support to students who do not receive sufficient financial aid from other sources.

The ACCESS committee stressed that students will be provided with information on an individual basis throughout the school year. Each student will be guided through the financial aid application and award process from beginning to end, so that he or she may take full advantage of all the financial aid available.

On April 2, 1985, New England Mutual Life Insurance Company announced a $1 million donation to start the ACCESS program.

With an additional $1 million challenge grant from the Boston Foundation, the Greater Boston business community now has set a goal of increasing ACCESS' endowment to $5 million. At that level, coupled with on-going fundraising, the business community hopes to assure every academically qualified student of Boston Public Schools enough financial assistance to continue their education upon graduation.

Getting the job done

In the first year of operation, 100 seniors received "last-dollar" scholarships averaging $500. Almost 1,000 seniors were counseled on obtaining financial help. In 1986, 150 students received funds averaging about $535 each.

At the heart of the ACCESS program is a group of financial aid advisors who will be at each of Boston's high schools working with seniors. They will:

• Provide information on higher education, stressing financial aid opportunities.

• Conduct workshops to develop an understanding of financial aid program requirements.

• Help seniors and their parents apply for post-secondary education and financial aid.

• Help needy students apply for ACCESS "last-dollar" scholarships.

The Boston Plan for Excellence in the Public Schools

ACCESS is a program of the Boston Plan for Excellence in the Public Schools, which also includes a School Grants Program funded by Bank of Boston; a Teacher Fellowship Program funded by the Bank of New England; and the Hancock Endowment for Academics, Recreation, and Teaching Program (HEART), which is supported by John Hancock.

ACCESS places financial aid advisors in each of the 17 Boston public high schools to assist students with planning for higher education and securing maximum financial aid from all other sources before turning to ACCESS funds. ACCESS then awards "last-dollar" scholarships to bridge the gap between a college student's resources and his or her needs.

Supported by the entire community, ACCESS is offering new hope to students who need help to cope with the difficult times ahead.

As School Committee Chairman John Nucci remarked: "At a time when tuitions are soaring and federal assistance programs are being cut back, ACCESS is a Godsend."

For more information on ACCESS contact:

Mario Pena, Executive Director
ACCESS, Boston Plan for Excellence
60 State Street
Boston, MA 02109
(617) 723-7489

The Higher Education Information Center Can Help You Reach Your Educational and Career Goals

What is the Higher Education Information Center?

The Higher Education Information Center offers free information and advice on educational, financial aid and career opportunities. The Center assists people of all ages who are interested in attending college, vocational school, graduate or professional school. Counselors at the Center specialize in identifying financial aid sources and can help complete financial aid applications. The Center also has a collection of occupational information for people interested in exploring careers.

Who can benefit from the Center's services?

- High school students and their parents
- Adults interested in returning to school
- Guidance counselors, teachers, and community agency representatives who need resource information
- Anyone interested in taking a course to develop particular skills
- Those interested in graduate or professional education
- People changing jobs who need career information

Can I afford to go to school if I don't have a lot of money?

Yes! There are many sources of financial aid to help you pay for tuition, fees, transportation, living expenses and child care.

We will help you find financial aid programs that you may be eligible for. We also can help you complete financial aid forms and provide you with an application fee waiver if you qualify.

How can the Center help me reach my educational goals?

Our counselors can help you:

- Select and apply to schools suited to your career interests
- Identify grants and loans to help pay for educational expenses
- Complete admissions and financial aid applications

What if I'm unsure about what I want to study?

Our counselors can help you consider various career possibilities. You can read our books and pamphlets on different occupations. The Center also has a short, computerized test which helps you match your interests with appropriate careers.

What if I didn't prepare for college in high school?

You can still attend college. We have information about special opportunities:

- Schools with open admissions policies and alternative entrance requirements
- Basic education programs to help you develop skills necessary to succeed in higher education
- Colleges that offer tutoring, counseling and other support services to help you achieve your goals

How do I use the Center's services?

Just visit or call us at one of our two offices. You don't need an appointment. A Spanish-speaking counselor is available. There is no charge for our services.

Main Office:	Boston Public Library 666 Boylston St. (Copley Square) Boston, MA (617) 536-0200
Hours:	Monday–Thursday, 9 a.m.–9 p.m. Friday & Saturday, 9 a.m.–5 p.m. Sunday, 2–6 p.m. (October–May)
Satellite Office:	Roxbury Area Planning Action Council 62 Warren St. (Dudley Square) Roxbury, MA (617) 442-5900
Hours:	Tuesday & Thursday, 9 a.m.–5 p.m.

What if I need assistance or information and live outside the Boston area?

Call our toll-free telephone hotline, the Career and Learning Line (CALL), at 1-800-442-1171. We will answer your questions and send you information, or refer you to schools and educational counseling services in your area.

The Higher Education Information Center, which includes the Boston Educational Opportunity Center, is a division of The Education Resources Institute. Major funding for the Center is provided by the U.S. Department of Education, 24 Boston area colleges, the Massachusetts Board of Regents, and Massachusetts Higher Education Assistance Corporation. The Boston Public Library and Roxbury Area Planning Action Council provide space for the Center's offices.

NOTE: These pages are reproduced from a 1986 HEIC publication.

GOALS OF THE MHEAC LOAN COUNSELING TASK FORCE

Overall Goal: To encourage professional, graduate, undergraduate and high schools to provide financial/debt management programs to meet the needs of their students. This will be accomplished by doing the following:

— Identifying people and materials available which could be used in financial/debt management workshops or courses. Emphasis will be placed on Massachusetts resources.

— Fostering working relationships between school and bank officials and providing them with the opportunity to plan jointly sponsored seminars.

— Disseminating model financial/debt management programs which already exist.

— Designing model financial/debt management curriculums which meet the needs of Massachusetts undergraduate and graduate school financial aid officers, high school guidance counselors and lenders.

— Planning and sponsoring a workshop for Massachusetts financial aid officers, bank officials, and guidance counselors which would publicize the availability of resource material and people, highlight model programs and bring school officials and bankers together in order to encourage them to jointly sponsor their own financial/debt management seminars or courses.

LOAN COUNSELING TASK FORCE INFORMATIONAL/EDUCATIONAL MODEL ONE

TARGET MARKETS

Themes	Prospective Borrowers	In-School Borrowers	Borrowers in Grace Period/ Repayment/Deferment/Default	Past Borrowers/Parents/ Legislators/Other
Educational Credit	Exhibit Art Competition Poster Series ————————————————————————————————→			
Alternatives to Borrowing	Brochures: "$Sources of Financial Aid" "Alternatives to Borrowing"			
How Much to Borrow	Poster: "Be A Wise Borrower" Brochure: "Borrower's Guide to Education Loan Programs"			
Application Process	Flipchart and Slide Show ——→ Audiovisual Production ——→			
Repayment	Brochure: "Life With a Student Loan: A Play With Different Endings"	Entrance and Exit Interview Materials — Educational Loans It's Your Choice	Repayment Hotline ————————————————→ Bank Stuffer Repayment Guide: "Everything You've Always Wanted to Know About Repaying Your GSL" Student Withdraw Brochure: "Changing Directions — What Happens to My Student Loan If My Plans Change" Borrowers Newsletter ————————————————→ Public Service Announcements Audiovisual/Production Credit Card	
Consequences of Default (All Themes)	←——— Speaker's Bureau ——→ ←——— Adult Learner Guide ——→ ←——— Media and Public Awareness Campaigns ——————————————————————————————————→ ←——— Promotional Items ——→ ←——— Higher Education Information Center ————————————————————————————————————→			

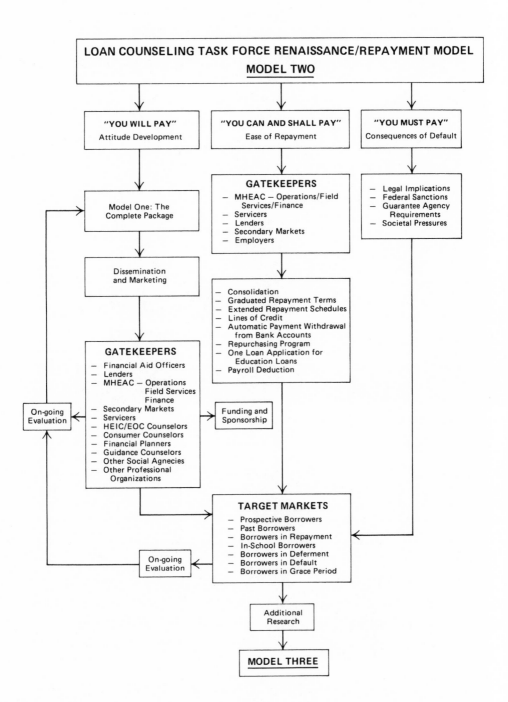

LOAN COUNSELING TASK FORCE RENAISSANCE/REPAYMENT MODEL
MODEL TWO

"YOU WILL PAY"
Attitude Development

"YOU CAN AND SHALL PAY"
Ease of Repayment

"YOU MUST PAY"
Consequences of Default

Model One: The
Complete Package

GATEKEEPERS
– MHEAC – Operations/Field
   Services/Finance
– Servicers
– Lenders
– Secondary Markets
– Employers

– Legal Implications
– Federal Sanctions
– Guarantee Agency
   Requirements
– Societal Pressures

Dissemination
and Marketing

– Consolidation
– Graduated Repayment Terms
– Extended Repayment Schedules
– Lines of Credit
– Automatic Payment Withdrawal
   from Bank Accounts
– Repurchasing Program
– One Loan Application for
   Education Loans
– Payroll Deduction

GATEKEEPERS
– Financial Aid Officers
– Lenders
– MHEAC – Operations
         Field Services
         Finance
– Secondary Markets
– Servicers
– HEIC/EOC Counselors
– Consumer Counselors
– Financial Planners
– Guidance Counselors
– Other Social Agnecies
– Other Professional
   Organizations

On-going
Evaluation

Funding and
Sponsorship

TARGET MARKETS
– Prospective Borrowers
– Past Borrowers
– Borrowers in Repayment
– In-School Borrowers
– Borrowers in Deferment
– Borrowers in Default
– Borrowers in Grace Period

On-going
Evaluation

Additional
Research

MODEL THREE

GLOSSARY OF TERMS

Accrued Interest: Interest which is earned on the loan and is payable by the borrower or the federal government. Each day interest is calculated on the unpaid principal balance and thus becomes "accrued interest."

Amortization: The gradual reduction of a loan debt by periodic installment (usually monthly) payments of principal and interest.

Consolidation: Combining one's loans by the process of selling and transferring all loans to one holder.

Cost of Education (or Cost of Attendance): The total amount it will cost a student to go to school, usually expressed as a yearly figure. For Pell grants, the cost of education is limited to tuition and fees; on-campus room and board; and allowances for books, supplies, and miscellaneous expenses. The campus-based and GSL programs are more flexible and may include other expenses such as travel, child care, and costs related to the needs of handicapped students. School financial aid administrators should be consulted about unusual expenses that may affect the cost of education or the student's ability to pay that cost.

Debt Burden: Total amount of money (principal and interest) which must be repaid.

Default: The failure of a borrower to make installment payments when due or to meet other terms of the promissory note, making it reasonable to conclude that the borrower no longer intends to honor the obligation to repay.

Deferment: An approved postponement of payment for a specified period.

Delinquency: Failure of the borrower to make an installment payment when due or to meet other terms of the promissory note.

Dependent Student: A student who does not qualify as an independent (see Independent Student).

Disbursement Date: The date the loan check is issued by the lender.

171

Discounted Loan: Loan on which the interest on a period calculated from disbursement to maturity is paid up front from the proceeds of the loan and the loan is paid in full at maturity.

Due Diligence: Requirement that a lender, in the servicing and collection of loans insured, use collection practices at least as extensive and forceful as those generally practiced by financial institutions for the collection of consumer loans.

Eligible Institution: An institution of higher education, a vocational school, or, with respect to students who are nationals of the United States, an institution outside the United States which is comparable to a U.S. institution of higher education or vocational school and which has been approved by the Secretary for the purpose of the guaranteed student loan program, except that such term does not include any such institution or school which employs or uses commission salesmen to promote the availability of any loan program described in section 428(a)(1), 428A, or 428B (of the Higher Education Act, as amended) at that institution or school.

Eligible Lender: The term "eligible lender" means:

(A) a National or State-chartered bank, a mutual savings bank, a savings and loan association, a stock savings bank, a trust company, or a credit union which:

    (i)   is subject to examination and supervision by an agency of the United States or of the State in which its principal place of operation is established, and

    (ii) does not have as its primary consumer credit function the making or holding of loans made to students under this part unless (I) it is a bank which is wholly owned by a State, (II) it is a single wholly owned subsidiary of a bank holding company which does not have as its primary consumer credit function the making or holding of loans made to students under the guaranteed student loan program, or (III) it is a trust company which makes student loans as a trustee pursuant to an express trust and which operated as a lender under this part prior to January 1, 1981;

(B) a pension fund as defined in the Employee Retirement Income Security Act;

(C) an insurance company which is subject to examination and supervision by an agency of the United States or a State;

(D) in any State, a single agency of the State or a single non-profit private agency designated by the State;

(E) an eligible institution which meets the requirements of paragraphs (2) through (5) of this subsection;

(F) for purposes only of purchasing and holding loans made by other lenders under this part, the Student Loan Marketing Association or an agency of any State functioning as a secondary market;

(G) for purposes of making loans under sections 428A(d), 428B(d), 428C, and 439(q) (of the Higher Education Act, as amended), the Student Loan Marketing Association;

(H) for purposes of making loans under sections 428(h) and 428(j) (of the Higher Education Act, as amended), a guaranty agency; and a Rural Rehabilitation Corporation, or its successor agency, which has received Federal funds under Public Law 499, Eighty-first Congress (64 Stat. 98 [1950]).

Expected Family Contribution: This figure is determined by a federal formula and indicates how much of a family's financial resources should be available to help pay for school. This figure is important because the financial aid administrator will subtract it from the cost of education to find out how much assistance is needed.

Financial Aid Package: The total amount of financial aid a student receives. Federal and non-federal aid such as loans, grants, scholarship, or work-study are combined in a "package" to help meet the student's need. Using available resources to give each student the best possible package of aid is one of the major responsibilities of a financial aid administrator.

Forbearance: Permitting the temporary cessation of principal payments or accepting lower payments than were previously agreed upon.

GSL: An educational loan subsidized by the federal government during periods of matriculation that are at a half-time or greater status and which are guaranteed and administered by a state agency for the federal government.

Grace Period: A six- or nine-month period before the borrower enters repayment.

Guarantee Agency: A state or private non-profit agency that administers a student loan insurance program—e.g., Massachusetts Higher Education Assistance Corporation (MHEAC).

Half-Time: At school's measuring progress by credit hours and academic terms, "half-time" means at least six semester hours or quarter hours per term. At schools measuring progress by credit hours but not using academic terms, "half-time" means at least 12 semester hours or 18 quarter hours per year. At schools measuring progress by clock hours, "half-time" means at least 12 hours per week.

Higher Education Act of 1965: Through Title IV of this Act, Congress authorized three types of student financial aid programs for higher education: grants, loans, and work.

Holder: An eligible lender who owns a loan; or the entity which holds a legally effective promissory note and which has the right to collect from the borrower.

Independent Student: The term "independent," when used with respect to a student, means an individual who meets one or more of the following criteria:

- Is 24 years of age or older by December 31 of the award year.
- Is a graduate, professional, or married student who declares that he/she will not be claimed as a dependent for income tax purposes by his/her parents (guardian) for the first calendar year of the award year.
- Has legal dependents other than a spouse.
- Is an orphan or ward of the court.
- Is a veteran of the United States Armed Forces.
- Is a student for which a financial aid administrator makes a documented determination of independence by reasons of other unusual circumstances.
- Is a single undergraduate student with no dependents who was not claimed as a dependent by his or her parents (or guardian) for income tax purposes for the two calendar years preceding the award year, and who demonstrates to the student financial aid administrator total self-sufficiency during the two calendar years preceding the award year in which the initial award will be granted by demonstrating an annual total income of $4,000.

Institution of Higher Education: An educational institution in any State which:

(1)   admits as regular students only persons having a certificate of graduation from a school providing secondary education, or the recognized equivalent of such certificate, or who are beyond the age of compulsory school attendance;

(2)   is legally authorized within such State to provide a program of education beyond secondary education;

(3)   provides an educational program for which it awards a bachelor's degree or provides not less than a 2-year program which is acceptable for full credit toward such a degree;

(4)   is a public or other nonprofit institution; and

(5)   is accredited by a nationally recognized accrediting agency or association approved by the Secretary for this purpose.

LCTF: Loan Counseling Task Force, a multi-agency professional group which develops materials to educate high school and college students about credit and the impact of debt on future lifestyle.

Line of Credit: The term "line of credit" means an arrangement or agreement between the lender and the borrower whereby a loan is paid out by the lender to the borrower in annual installments, or whereby the lender agrees to make, in addition to the initial loan, additional loans in subsequent years.

Loan Maturity: The date a loan becomes due for repayment, subsequent to a grace period following completion of schooling.

Loan Origination: All of the steps required to initiate a loan from application to final approval.

Maker: The borrower.

Market Rate: Interest rate based upon indicators that are sensitive to the daily money exchanges—Prime interest rate, Treasury Bill (T-Bill), Treasury Note (T-Note), Federal Discount, etc.

NCHELP: The National Council of Higher Education Loan Programs, a professional association for guarantee agencies, secondary markets, lenders, servicers, and others interested in educational lending.

NDSL: National Direct Student Loan (now called the Carl D. Perkins Loan).

Need Analysis: The process of determining a student's eligibility for financial aid. Income and asset information from both the student and parents is examined to determine the family's ability to contribute toward educational costs. This figure, called the expected family contribution, is subtracted from what it will cost the student to attend a given institution for a specific length of time (typically one academic year). If the college's cost of attendance is more than the family can contribute, the student has financial need and is usually eligible for financial aid equal to the amount of his or her demonstrated financial need.

Offset: To transfer funds in order to partially or fully retire a debt.

Origination Fee: Fee used by the federal government to offset its cost in the GSL program. It may be subtracted from the proceeds of the loan and is subject to changes due to action by the Congress.

Parental Leave: The term "parental leave" means a period:
(1) during which the borrower is pregnant, caring for his or her newborn child, or caring for his or her child immediately following the placement of the child through adoption;
(2) during which such borrower is not in attendance at an eligible institution or gainfully employed; and
(3) which follows, by 6 months or less, a period during which the borrower was enrolled in at least a half-time course of study at an eligible institution.

Pell: Formerly the Basic Educational Opportunity Grant (BEOG).

PLUS: A variable rate loan not to exceed 12 percent, available to parents of dependent students.

Promissory Note: The legal document signed when one receives a student loan. It lists the conditions for borrowing and the terms under which the loan is to be paid back.

Proprietary School: Owner-operated school.

Reauthorization: The re-empowerment of the Higher Education Act by the Congress.

Secondary Market: A state or private agency that purchases GSL and PLUS loans from lenders.

SEOG: Supplementary Educational Opportunity Grant.

Servicer: The entity designated to track and collect a loan on behalf of the holder.

Student Supplemental Loan: A variable rate loan not to exceed 12 percent.

Vocational School: The term "vocational school" means a business or trade school, or a technical institution or other technical or vocational school, in any State, which:

   (1)   admits as regular students only persons who have completed or left elementary or secondary school and who have the ability to benefit (as determined by the institution under section 481[d]) (of the Higher Education Act, as amended) from the training offered by such institution;

   (2)   is legally authorized to provide, and provides within that State, a program of postsecondary vocational or technical education designed to fit individuals for useful employment in recognized occupations;

   (3)   has been in existence for two years or has been specially accredited by the Secretary.

BIBLIOGRAPHY

American Council on Education. *Fact Sheet: Student Borrowing Has Implications for Career Choice*. Washington, D.C., August 1985.

Anderson, Britta. *A Study of Defaulted Borrowers in Vermont, 1965 to 1981*. Winooski, Vermont: Vermont Student Assistance Corporation, 1983.

Anderson, Raymond B., and Allen R. Sanderson. *Financial Issues in Graduate Education and an Agenda for Research Public Law 96-374, 7(A)*. Washington, D.C.: National Commission on Student Financial Assistance, 1982.

Arbeiter, Solomon. "Minority Enrollment in Higher Education Institutions: A Chronological View," *Research and Development Update*. New York: The College Board, May 1986.

Astin, Alexander W. "The Impact of Student Financial Aid Programs on Student Choice," *Final Report, SISFAP–Study A*. U.S. Office of Education (n.d.–1978?), p. 5.

Axt, Richard G. *The Federal Government and Financing Higher Education*. New York: Columbia University Press, 1952.

Bargar, Gwyneth, and Harold Bargar. *College on Credit: A History of United States Student Aid Funds: 1960–1980*. Indianapolis: Hackett Publishing Company, 1981.

Boyd, Joseph D., and J. Martin. *The NASFAA Loan Study: A Report on the Characteristics of GSL Borrowers and the Impact of Educational Debt*. Washington, D.C.: National Association of Student Financial Aid Administrators, 1986.

Boyd, Joseph D. *Guaranteed Student Loan Program, GSL-2: State by State Report/Comparative Study of Self-Reported Data from Guaranty Agency Federal Quarterly Reports, Federal Fiscal Year and Cumulative Status as of September 30, 1983 and 1984*. Deerfield, Illinois: Joseph D. Boyd and Associates, 1985.

Boyd, Joseph D., and Dennis Martin. *The Impact of Educational Loan Debt on Borrowers' Personal Life Decisions*. Washington, D.C.: National Association of Student Financial Aid Administrators, September 1985 (draft version), p. 56.

Brock, David. "Banks Push Loans to College Students," *Wall Street Journal*, August 20, 1985, p. 27.

California Guaranteed Student Loan Program. "Default Statistics by Educational Segments." Sacramento, California: California Student Aid Commission, 1984 (mimeographed report).

California Postsecondary Education Commission. *Mortgaging a Generation: Problems and Prospects of California's Guaranteed Student Loan Program*. Sacramento, California: The Commission, 1985.

California Student Aid Commission. *Mortgaging a Generation: Problems and Prospects of the California Guaranteed Student Loan Program*. Sacramento, California: Postsecondary Education Commission, March 1985.

Carnegie Foundation for the Advancement of Teaching. "Change Trendlines: The Price of College Shaping Students' Choices." *Change*, Volume 18, Number 3, May/June 1986, pp. 27–30.

Caro, Robert A. *The Years of Lyndon Johnson: The Path to Power*. New York: Vintage Books, 1983.

Cattie, Eugene G., Executive Director, Virginia Education Loan Authority. Testimony before House Subcommittee on Postsecondary Education, June 19, 1985. Several other presenters that day and on June 5 made similar recommendations. See "Report to Accompany H.R. 3700, Higher Education Amendments of 1985," House of Representatives Report 99-383, November 20, 1985, pp. 35–42.

Cheskis-Gold, Rena. "The Yale TPO/CRO Loan Experience: A 1983 Survey of TPO/CRO Borrowers." Yale University Office of Institutional Research, report 84R001, August 1984.

College Board New York Office. *Keeping the Options Open. Recommendations. Final Report of the Commission on Precollege Guidance and Counseling*. New York: College Entrance Examination Board, 1986.

College Board Washington Office. *Trends in Student Aid: 1980 to 1986*. New York: The College Board, 1986.

College Board Washington Office. *Who Receives Federal Student Aid?* Washington, D.C.: The College Board, February 1986.

College Scholarship Service. *Proceedings: College Scholarship Service Colloquium on Student Loan Counseling and Debt Management*. New York: College Entrance Examination Board, 1986.

College Scholarship Service and National Association of Student Financial Aid Administrators. *Survey of Undergraduate Financial Aid Policies, Practices and Procedures*. Forthcoming.

Council of Teaching Hospitals Survey of House Staff Stipends. Washington, D.C.: Association of American Medical Colleges, 1982 (Table 2).

Coury, John J. "Educational Indebtedness and the Career Choices of New Physicians." Chicago, Illinois: American Medical Association, 1983, Report E(I-83).

Credit Research Center. *The Role of Education Debt in Consumers' Total Debt Structure*. Lafayette: Purdue University, 1983.

Daniere, Andre. "The Benefits and Costs of Alternative Federal Programs of Financial Aid to College Students," in *The Economics and Financing of Higher Education in the United States: A Compendium of Papers Submitted to the Joint Economic Committee*. Washington, D.C.: U.S. Government Printing Office, 1969, pp. 576–578.

Davis, Jerry. "Paying for College Costs: Does the Student's Sex Make a Difference?" *Journal of Student Financial Aid*, November 1977, Ch. 7, pp. 21–34.

Davis, Jerry S. *Guaranteed Student Loan Program Default Rates and Volumes by States for Fiscal Years 1981, 1982, and 1983*. Harrisburg, Pennsylvania: Pennsylvania Higher Education Assistance Agency, 1984.

Davis, Jerry S. *What Our Alumni Have Done: A Study of the Employment and Educational Activities of Pennsylvania State Grant Recipients One Year After Completion of Their Undergraduate Program, Spring, 1982*. Harrisburg, Pennsylvania: Pennsylvania Higher Education Assistance Agency, 1983.

Davis, Jerry S. "Ten Facts About Defaults in the Guaranteed Student Loan Program." Testimony before House Subcommittee on Postsecondary Education, June 19, 1985. See also Hauptman, Arthur M. "Student Loan Default Rates in Perspective." American Council on Education Policy Brief. Washington, D.C., February 1983.

Davis, Jerry S. "GSL Borrower Characteristics." Report to the Second Annual NASSGP/NCHELP Research Conference, Washington, D.C., May 31, 1985.

Davis, Jerry S. "Growing by Leaps and Bounds: A Study of Guaranteed Student Loan Program Indebtedness of Pennsylvania Postsecondary Students, 1974–75 to 1983–84." Harrisburg, Pennsylvania: Pennsylvania Higher Education Assistance Authority, mimeograph, November 1985.

Dennis, Marguerite J. An Expanded View of the Role of the Financial Aid Administrator in Student Debt Management. *Journal of Student Financial Aid*, 1983, 13 (3), 33–38.

Dennis, Marguerite J. *Mortgaged Futures: How to Graduate from School Without Going Broke*. Washington, D.C.: Hope Press, 1986.

Department of Health and Human Services. *A Protocol for Teaching Fiscal Planning and Management to Health Professions and Nursing Students*. Handout #10, Student Financial Aid Training Conference, Chicago, Illinois, April 1985.

Doyle, Denis P., and Terry W. Hartle. "Facing the Fiscal Chopping Block: It's Time to Rethink Student Aid." *Change*, July/August 1985, p. 8ff. See also McPherson, op. cit., pp. 25–30.

Dresch, Stephen, with Bruce Johnstone. *New Patterns for College Lending*. New York and London: Columbia University Press, 1972.

Dresch, Stephen. "The Educational Credit Trust: A Proposal for Reconstitution and Reform of the Student Loan System." Sacramento, California: The Sequoia Institute, 1983.

Ehlenfeldt, Lisa L., and Donna Springfield. *Study of Guaranteed Student Loan Defaults*. Richmond, Virginia: Virginia Education Loan Authority, 1984.

El-Khawas, Elaine. *Better Information for Student Choice: A Report of a National Task Force*. Washington, D.C.: American Association for Higher Education, 1977.

Felmeister, C. J., and M. M. Tulman. *Mosby's Dental Practice Management Series, Personalized Guide to Financial Planning*. St. Louis: The C. V. Mosby Company, 1983.

Fenske, Robert, James Hearn, and Denis Curry. *Unmet Student Financial Need in the State of Washington: A Study of the "Need Gap."* Olympia: State of Washington Council for Postsecondary Education, 1985.

Fishbein, Estelle A., and Dennis H. Blumer. *Report of the Task Force on De-Regulation Initiatives*. Washington, D.C.: National Association of College and University Attorneys, 1981.

Flamer, Herbert J., and Dwight H. Horch. *Talented and Needy Graduate and Professional Students: A National Survey of People Who Applied for Need-Based Financial Aid to Attend Graduate or Professional School in 1980–81*. Princeton, N.J.: Educational Testing Service, 1982.

Frances, Carol. "1986: Major Trends Shaping the Outlook for Higher Education." *AAHE Bulletin*, December 1985, p. 5.

Frances, op. cit., pp. 4–5. See also Christoffel, Pamela. *Working Your Way Through College: A New Look at an Old Idea*. Washington, D.C.: The College Board, October, 1985.

Froomkin, Joseph. "Study of the Advantages and Disadvantages of Loans to Women." Prepared for the U.S. Department of Health, Education, and Welfare, December 1974.

Gillespie, Donald A., and Nancy Carlson. *Trends in Student Aid: 1963 to 1983*. New York: The College Board, 1983.

Gillespie, Donald A., and Nancy Carlson. *Trends in Student Aid: 1963 to 1983*. Washington, D.C.: The College Board, 1983, Table A-4, p. 35.

Gillespie, Donald A., and Lynn Quincy. *Trends in Student Aid: 1980 to 1984*. Washington, D.C.: The College Board, 1984, Table 4, pg. 7.

Gladieux, Lawrence E., Janet S. Hansen, and Mark L. Wolfe. *Issues and Options in the Guaranteed Student Loan Program*. Washington, D.C.: The College Board, 1985, page 5.

Guthrie, Marty, and Renee Rappaport. *A Guide to Disbursement, Refund, and Repayment*. Washington, D.C.: Office of Student Financial Assistance, 1984.

Halloran, Michael H. "Commentary." College Scholarship Service *Proceedings* (see above), 1986.

Hansen, W. Lee, and Marilyn Rhodes. *Student Debt Crisis: Are Students Incurring Excessive Debt?* Madison: Wisconsin Center for Educational Research, October 1985.

Hansen, Janet S., and Paul L. Franklin. *College Opportunity and Public Assistance Programs: Ideas for Resolving Conflicts*. Washington, D.C.: The College Board, 1984.

Hansen, Janet S. "The Politics of Federal Scholarships: A Case Study of the Development of General Grant Assistance for Undergraduates." Ph.D. dissertation, Princeton University, February 1977.

Hartle, Terry, and Richard Wabnick. *Discretionary Income and College Costs*. Washington, D.C.: National Commission on Student Financial Assistance, 1982.

Hartle, Terry, and Richard Wabnick. *The Educational Indebtedness of Graduate and Professional Students*. Washington, D.C.: Educational Testing Service, 1983.

Hartman, Robert W. *Credit for College*. New York: McGraw Hill, 1971, p. 14.

Hartman, Robert W. *Credit for College: Public Policy for Student Loans*. A Report for the Carnegie Commission on Higher Education, 1971.

Hastings, Richard, Director—Office of Debt Collection and Management, U.S. Department of Education. Statement before House Subcommittee on Oversight. Committee on Ways and Means, September 19, 1985, p. 3.

Hauptman, Arthur M. *Student Loan Default Rates in Perspective*, ACE Policy Brief. Washington, D.C.: American Council on Education, 1983.

Hauptman, Arthur. *Federal Costs for Student Loans: Is There a Role for Institution-Based Lending?* Washington, D.C.: American Council on Education, June 1985. See also Douma, Wallace H. *Improving the Student Financial Aid System to Provide Efficiency for Taxpayers*. Madison: Wisconsin Center for Educational Research, October 1985.

Hauptman, Arthur M. *Financing Student Loans: The Search for Alternatives in the Face of Federal Contraction*. Washington, D.C.: The College Board, 1982, p. 2.

Hauptman, Arthur M. "National Student Loan Bank: The Road Less Traveled." National Association of Independent Colleges and Universities agenda materials for tenth annual meeting, February 1986a.

Hauptman, Arthur M. *Students in Graduate and Professional Education: What We Know and Need to Know*. Washington, D.C.: Association of American Universities, 1986b.

Hearn, James C., and Sharon L. Wilford. *A Commitment to Opportunity: The Impacts of Federal Student Financial Aid Programs*. Report prepared for the 20th Anniversary Observance of the Signing of the Higher Education Act of 1965, Southwest Texas State University, San Marcos, Texas, November 1985. See also McPherson, op. cit., pp. 4–20.

Hesseldenz, Jon S., and David Stockham. "National Direct Student Loan Defaulters: The Ability to Repay," *Research in Higher Education*. Association for Institutional Research, 1982.

Hills, Donald E., and William D. Van Dusen. *A Report on the Expenses of Undergraduate Students Enrolled in California Postsecondary Institutions During the 1982–83 Academic Year*. Sacramento: California Student Aid Commission, 1985.

Horch, Dwight H. *Estimating Manageable Educational Loan Limits for Graduate and Professional Students*. Princeton, N.J.: Educational Testing Service, 1982.

Horch, Dwight H. "Critique of the Proposal for an Educational Credit Trust." Princeton, N.J.: Educational Testing Service, 1983 (mimeograph).

Horch, Dwight H. *Student Loan Limits: Estimated Manageable Student Loan Limits for the Class Graduating in 1984 and the Class Entering in 1985*. Princeton, N.J.: Educational Testing Service, 1984.

Horch, Dwight H., with H. J. Flamer. *Talented and Needy Graduate and Professional Students: A National Survey of People Who Applied for Need-Based Financial Aid to Attend Graduate or Professional School in 1980–81*. Princeton, N.J.: Educational Testing Service, 1982.

Hornig, Lilli. Testimony before the National Commission on Student Financial Assistance, Subcommittee on Graduate Education, at New York University, March 15, 1983. Washington, D.C.: National Archives.

House Subcommittee on Postsecondary Education, Hearings on "Debt Burdens, Loan Limits, Needs Analysis, Income Caps," June 5, 1985. Testimony of Charles Saunders and William J. Sullivan, SJ.

Illinois State Scholarship Commission. "Characteristics of Illinois Borrowers Who Defaulted on Illinois Guaranteed Student Loans, 1967 to 1982," Springfield, Illinois: The Commission, 1983.

Illinois Board of Higher Education and Illinois State Scholarship Commission. *Student Financial Aid by Source, Type, Sector, and Level During Fiscal Year 1985*. Springfield, Illinois, April 1986.

Jensen, Eric L. "Financial Aid and Educational Outcomes: A Review." *College and University*, Spring, 1983, pp. 287–302.

Johnson, Robert W., and A. Charlene Sullivan. *The Role of Education Debt in Consumers' Total Debt Structure*. West Lafayette, Indiana: Purdue University, Krannert Graduate School of Management Credit Research Center, Working paper number 45, 1983.

Johnstone, D. Bruce. *Sharing the Costs of Higher Education: Student Financial Assistance in the United Kingdom, the Federal Republic of Germany, France, Sweden, and the United States*. New York: The College Board, 1986.

Klein, Susan S. *Handbook for Achieving Sex Equity through Education*. Baltimore: Johns Hopkins University Press, ed. 1985.

Lee, John B. *Study of Guaranteed Student Loan Default Rates*. Washington, D.C.: Applied Systems Institute, Inc., 1982.

Leider, Robert. *Student's Guide to Scholarships and Loans*. Alexandria, Va.: Octameron Press, 1983.

Levy, Frank S., and Richard C. Michel. "The Economic Future of the Baby Boom." Paper prepared under contract with the Joint Economic Committee of the U.S. Congress, mimeograph, December 1985.

Lindquist, Victor R., and Frank S. Endicott. *Northwestern Endicott Report for 1984*. Evanston, Illinois: Northwestern University, 1983.

Litten, Larry. Telephone conversation with the author, July 1986.

Little, Kathleen W. "Commentary." College Scholarship Service *Proceedings* (see above), 1986.

Luckett, Charles A., and James D. August. "The Growth of Consumer Debt." *Federal Reserve Bulletin*, Volume 71, Number 6, pp. 389–402, June 1985.

Marchese, Theodore J. "Five Articles, One Tough Issue." *Change*, Volume 18, Number 3, May/June 1986a, pp. 1–5.

Marchese, Theodore J. "Fulfilling the Institution's Responsibilities to Student Borrowers." College Scholarship Service *Proceedings* (see above), 1986.

Martin, Dennks J. "Long-Term Implications of Student Borrowing." College Scholarship Service *Proceedings* (see above), 1986.

McAlvey, Warren C. *A Guide to the Repayment of Multiple National Direct Student Loans*. Washington, D.C.: Office of Student Financial Assistance, 1984.

McAlvey, Warren C., and Anne J. Price. *Student Loan Collection Procedures*. Washington, D.C.: National Association of College and University Business Officers, 1985.

McPherson, Michael S. "Federal Student Aid Policy: Can We Learn from Experience?" Washington, D.C.: The Brookings Institution, mimeograph, October 1985.

McPherson, Michael S. *How Can We Tell If Federal Student Aid Is Working?* Washington, D.C.: The College Board, Forthcoming.

Miller, Scott E. *The National Commission on Student Financial Assistance: A Summary of Its Recommendations*, Policy Brief. Washington, D.C.: American Council on Education, 1984.

Miller, Scott E. *Student and Parent Loans: A Growing Reliance*. Washington, D.C.: American Council on Education, 1985.

Miller, Scott, and Holly Hexter. *How Low-Income Families Pay for College*. Washington, D.C.: American Council on Education, July 1985, pp. 11 and 17.

Miller, Scott, and Holly Hexter. *How Middle-Income Families Pay for College*. Washington, D.C.: American Council on Education, 1985.

Moran, Mary. *Student Financial Aid and Women: Equity Dilemma?* Washington, D.C.: Association for the Study of Higher Education, 1987.

Myers, G., and S. Siera. "Development and Validation of Discriminant Analysis Models for Student Loan Defaulters and Non-Defaulters." *Journal of Student Financial Aid*, Vol. 10, No. 1, NASFAA, 1980.

National Association of Student Financial Aid Administrators. *Stages in the Development of a Financial Counseling and Debt Management Model*. Washington, D.C.: NASFAA Monograph Series, Number V, July, 1984.

National Commission on Student Financial Assistance. *Guaranteed Student Loans: A Background Paper*. Washington, D.C.: The National Commission, 1982.

National Commission on Student Financial Assistance. *The Role of Educational Debt in Consumers' Total Debt Structure*. Washington, D.C.: The National Commission, 1983.

National Council of Higher Education Loan Programs. *State Agency Survey: Guaranteed Education Loan Programs*, 1984. Albany, New York: New York State Higher Education Services Corporation, 1985.

National Council of Higher Education Loan Programs. *Introduction to the Guaranteed Student Loan Program*. Washington, D.C., NCHELP, 1985.

National Institute of Education. *Involvement in Learning*. Washington, D.C.: NIE, October 1984, pp. 25–26.

National Survey of Professional Administrative, Technical, and Cleri-

cal Pay, March 1982. Washington, D.C.: U.S. Department of Labor, Department of Labor Statistics, Bulletin Number 2145, 1982.

Newman, Frank. *Higher Education and the American Resurgence.* Princeton, N.J.: The Carnegie Foundation for the Advancement of Teaching, 1985, Table 6, p. 75.

New York State Higher Education Services Corporation, *Student Loan Payers and Defaulters.* Albany, New York: New York State Higher Education Services Corporation, 1985.

Orr, Theresa. *Reasonable Loan Limits: What Are They?* Paper presented at the meeting of the National Association of Student Financial Aid Administrators, Washington, D.C., July 1985.

Pearce, Douglas K. "Rising Household Debt in Perspective." *Economic Review,* Volume 70, Number 7, pp. 3–17, July/August 1985.

Popik, Roberta. "Å Model for Estimating Manageable Debt Principals." Evanston, Ill.: Northwestern University (mimeo), August 21, 1983.

Reynolds, Roger A., and Jonathan B. Abram. *Socioeconomic Characteristics of Medical Practice, 1983.* Chicago, Illinois: American Medical Association, 1983 (Table 40).

Rosenfeld, Rachel A., and James C. Hearn. "Sex Differences in the Significance of Economic Resources for Choosing and Attending a College," in *The Undergraduate Woman: Issues in Education Equity,* edited by P. Perena. Lexington, Massachusetts: Lexington Books, 1982.

Sanford, Timothy R. "Residual Effects of Self-Help on the Lives of College Graduates." *Journal of Student Financial Aid,* Vol. 9, No. 3, NASFAA, 1979.

Signs of Trouble and Erosion: A Report on Graduate Education in America. Washington, D.C.: Subcommittee on Graduate Education, National Commission on Student Financial Assistance, 1983.

Spero, Irene K. *The Use of Student Financial Aid to Attract Prospective Teachers: A Survey of State Efforts,* Washington, D.C.: The College Board, 1986.

Stampen, Jacob O., and Albert F. Cabrera. *Is the Student Aid System Achieving Its Objectives? Evidence on Targeting and Attrition.* Madison: Wisconsin Center for Educational Research, October 1985. See also Wellford W. Wilms. *Successfully Targeting Federal Student Aid: The GSL Program and Vocational Students.* Santa Monica: Training Research Corp., December 18, 1984.

Stanley, David T., and Marjorie Girth. *Bankruptcy: Problem, Process, Reform.* Washington, D.C.: The Brookings Institute, 1971.

Stedman, James B. "The Cumulative Educational Debt of Postsecondary Students: Amounts and Measures of Manageability." Washington, D.C.: Congressional Research Service, Library of Congress, mimeograph, 1984.

Stickney, John. "The Class of 2000: Paying the Price." *Washington Post*, November 19, 1985, p. E5.

"Student Financial Aid in the UW (University of Wisconsin) System: Status, Trends, and Analysis." Mimeograph, n.d.

Sullivan, A. Charlene. "Consumer Credit: Are There Limits?" West Lafayette, Indiana: Purdue University, mimeograph, 1986.

Terrell, Charles, and others. *Financing Medical Education, 1982–1983*. Washington, D.C.: National Association of Medical Minority Educators, 1982.

Three Standards of Living for an Urban Family of Four Persons. Washington, D.C.: U.S. Department of Labor, Bureau of Labor Statistics, Bulletin Number 1570–5, 1967.

Thrift, Julianne Still, and Christopher M. Toppe. *Paying for College: Trends in Student Financial Aid at Independent Colleges and Universities*. Washington, D.C.: National Institute of Independent Colleges and Universities, 1985, p. 3.

Tombaugh, R., and W. Troutman. "Student Attitudes Toward Borrowing and Working—Results of National Surveys." *College and University*, Vol. 47, No. 4 (1972), pp. 439–441.

Touche Ross and Company. *Study of the Insurance Premium Charged to Borrowers Under the Guaranteed Student Loan Program*. Washington, D.C., 1983.

U.S. Department of Education. "The High School and Beyond Data," 83-9-8. Washington, D.C.: National Center for Education Statistics, Longitudinal Studies Branch, 1983.

U.S. Department of Education, *Guaranteed Student Loan Program Data Book, FY 1984*. Washington, D.C.: Guaranteed Student Loan Branch, Division of Policy and Program Development, OSFA, 1985.

Voorhees, Richard A. "Financial Aid and Persistence: Do the Federal Campus-Based Programs Make a Difference?" *Journal of Student Financial Aid*. Volume 15, Number 1, pp. 21–30, Winter 1985.

Wabnick, Richard, and William Goggin. *Indebtedness to Finance Postsecondary Education*. Princeton, N.J.: Educational Testing Service, 1981.

Williams, Gareth. "The Economic Approach," Burton R. Clark, ed., *Perspectives on Higher Education: Eight Disciplinary and Comparative Views*. Berkeley: University of California Press, pp. 79–103, 1984.

Wilms, Wellford W. *Proprietary and Vocational Schools and Federal*

Student Aid: Opportunities for the Disadvantaged. Washington, D.C.: National Commission on Student Financial Aid, 1983.

Wilson, Robin. "U.S. to Survey College Students, Parents to Build Financial Aid Data Bank." *Chronicle of Higher Education,* November 27, 1985, p. 15.

INDEX

189